MW00984940

The Law School Admission Council (LSAC) is a nonprofit corporation that provides unique, state-of-the-art admission products and services to ease the admission process for law schools and their applicants worldwide. Currently, 221 law schools in the United States, Canada, and Australia are members of the Council and benefit from LSAC's services.

LSAT, Law School Admission Test, *The Official LSAT PrepTest*, *The Official LSAT SuperPrep*, *ItemWise*, and LSAC are registered marks of the Law School Admission Council, Inc. Law School Forums, LLM Law School Forum, Credential Assembly Service, CAS, LLM Credential Assembly Service, and LLM CAS are service marks of the Law School Admission Council, Inc. *10 Actual, Official LSAT PrepTests*; *10 More Actual, Official LSAT PrepTests*; *The Next 10 Actual, Official LSAT PrepTests*; *10 Actual Official LSAT PrepTests 42–51*; *10 New Actual, Official LSAT PrepTests with Comparative Reading*; *10 Actual, Official LSAT PrepTests, Volume V*; *The Official LSAT SuperPrep II*; LSAC Official Guide to ABA-Approved Law Schools; LSAC Official Guide to LLM/Graduate Law Programs; *The Official LSAT Handbook*; ACES²; FlexApp; Candidate Referral Service; DiscoverLaw.org; Law School Admission Test; and Law School Admission Council are trademarks of the Law School Admission Council, Inc.

LSAC fees, policies, and procedures relating to, but not limited to, test registration, test administration, test score reporting, misconduct and irregularities, Credential Assembly Service (CAS), and other matters may change without notice at any time. Up-to-date LSAC policies and procedures are available at LSAC.org.

ISBN-13: 978-0-9983397-6-4

Print number
10 9 8 7 6 5 4 3 2 1

TABLE OF CONTENTS

INTRODUCTION TO THE LSAT

The Law School Admission Test is a half-day standardized test required for admission to all ABA-approved law schools, most Canadian law schools, and many other law schools. It consists of five 35-minute sections of multiple-choice questions. Four of the five sections contribute to the test taker's score. These sections include one Reading Comprehension section, one Analytical Reasoning section, and two Logical Reasoning sections. The unscored section, commonly referred to as the variable section, typically is used to pretest new test questions or to preequate new test forms. The placement of this section in the LSAT will vary. A 35-minute writing sample is administered at the end of the test. The writing sample is not scored by LSAC, but copies are sent to all law schools to which you apply. The score scale for the LSAT is 120 to 180.

The LSAT is designed to measure skills considered essential for success in law school: the reading and comprehension of complex texts with accuracy and insight; the organization and management of information and the ability to draw reasonable inferences from it; the ability to think critically; and the analysis and evaluation of the reasoning and arguments of others.

The LSAT provides a standard measure of acquired reading and verbal reasoning skills that law schools can use as one of several factors in assessing applicants.

For up-to-date information about LSAC's services, go to our website, LSAC.org.

SCORING

Your LSAT score is based on the number of questions you answer correctly (the raw score). There is no deduction for incorrect answers, and all questions count equally. In other words, there is no penalty for guessing.

Test Score Accuracy—Reliability and Standard Error of Measurement

Candidates perform at different levels on different occasions for reasons quite unrelated to the characteristics of a test itself. The accuracy of test scores is best described by the use of two related statistical terms: reliability and standard error of measurement.

Reliability is a measure of how consistently a test measures the skills being assessed. The higher the reliability coefficient for a test, the more certain we can be that test takers would get very similar scores if they took the test again.

LSAC reports an internal consistency measure of reliability for every test form. Reliability can vary from 0.00 to 1.00, and a test with no measurement error would have a reliability coefficient of 1.00 (never attained in practice). Reliability coefficients for past LSAT forms have ranged from .90 to .95, indicating a high degree of consistency for these tests. LSAC expects the reliability of the LSAT to continue to fall within the same range.

LSAC also reports the amount of measurement error associated with each test form, a concept known as the standard error of measurement (SEM). The SEM, which is usually about 2.6 points, indicates how close a test taker's observed score is likely to be to his or her true score. True scores are theoretical scores that would be obtained from perfectly reliable tests with no measurement error—scores never known in practice.

Score bands, or ranges of scores that contain a test taker's true score a certain percentage of the time, can be derived using the SEM. LSAT score bands are constructed by adding and subtracting the (rounded) SEM to and from an actual LSAT score (e.g., the LSAT score, plus or minus 3 points). Scores near 120 or 180 have asymmetrical bands. Score bands constructed in this manner will contain an individual's true score approximately 68 percent of the time.

Measurement error also must be taken into account when comparing LSAT scores of two test takers. It is likely that small differences in scores are due to measurement error rather than to meaningful differences in ability. The standard error of score differences provides some guidance as to the importance of differences between two scores. The standard error of score differences is approximately 1.4 times larger than the standard error of measurement for the individual scores.

Thus, a test score should be regarded as a useful but approximate measure of a test taker's abilities as measured by the test, not as an exact determination of his or her abilities. LSAC encourages law schools to examine the range of scores within the interval that probably contains the test taker's true score (e.g., the test taker's score band) rather than solely interpret the reported score alone.

Adjustments for Variation in Test Difficulty

All test forms of the LSAT reported on the same score scale are designed to measure the same abilities, but one test form may be slightly easier or more difficult than another. The scores from different test forms are made comparable through a statistical procedure known as equating. As a result of equating, a given scaled score earned on different test forms reflects the same level of ability.

Research on the LSAT

Summaries of LSAT validity studies and other LSAT research can be found in member law school libraries and at LSAC.org.

To Inquire About Test Questions

If you find what you believe to be an error or ambiguity in a test question that affects your response to the question, contact LSAC by e-mail: LSATTS@LSAC.org, or write to Law School Admission Council, Test Development Group, PO Box 40, Newtown, PA 18940-0040.

HOW THIS PREPTEST DIFFERS FROM AN ACTUAL LSAT

This PrepTest is made up of the scored sections and writing sample from the actual disclosed LSAT administered in December 2017. However, it does not contain the extra, variable section that is used to pretest new test items of one of the three multiple-choice question types. The three multiple-choice question types may be in a different order in an actual LSAT than in this PrepTest. This is because the order of these question types is intentionally varied for each administration of the test.

THE THREE LSAT MULTIPLE-CHOICE QUESTION TYPES

The multiple-choice questions that make up most of the LSAT reflect a broad range of academic disciplines and are intended to give no advantage to candidates from a particular academic background.

The five sections of the test contain three different question types. The following material presents a general discussion of the nature of each question type and some strategies that can be used in answering them.

Analytical Reasoning Questions

Analytical Reasoning questions are designed to assess the ability to consider a group of facts and rules, and, given those facts and rules, determine what could or must be true. The specific scenarios associated with these questions are usually unrelated to law, since they are intended to be accessible to a wide range of test takers. However, the skills tested parallel those involved in determining what could or must be the case given a set of regulations, the terms of a contract, or the facts of a legal case in relation to the law. In Analytical Reasoning questions, you are asked to reason deductively from a set of statements and rules or principles that describe relationships among persons, things, or events.

Analytical Reasoning questions appear in sets, with each set based on a single passage. The passage used for each set of questions describes common ordering relationships or grouping relationships, or a combination of both types of relationships. Examples include scheduling employees for work shifts, assigning instructors to class sections, ordering tasks according to priority, and distributing grants for projects.

Analytical Reasoning questions test a range of deductive reasoning skills. These include:

- Comprehending the basic structure of a set of relationships by determining a complete solution to the problem posed (for example, an acceptable seating arrangement of all six diplomats around a table)

- Reasoning with conditional ("if-then") statements and recognizing logically equivalent formulations of such statements

- Inferring what could be true or must be true from given facts and rules

- Inferring what could be true or must be true from given facts and rules together with new information in the form of an additional or substitute fact or rule

- Recognizing when two statements are logically equivalent in context by identifying a condition or rule that could replace one of the original conditions while still resulting in the same possible outcomes

Analytical Reasoning questions reflect the kinds of detailed analyses of relationships and sets of constraints that a law student must perform in legal problem solving. For example, an Analytical Reasoning passage might describe six diplomats being seated around a table, following certain rules of protocol as to who can sit where. You, the test taker, must answer questions about the logical implications of given and new information. For example, you may be asked who can sit between diplomats X and Y, or who cannot sit next to X if W sits next to Y. Similarly, if you were a student in law school, you might be asked to analyze a scenario involving a set of particular circumstances and a set of governing rules in the form of constitutional provisions, statutes, administrative codes, or prior rulings that have been upheld. You might then be asked to determine the legal options in the scenario: what is required given the scenario, what is permissible given the scenario, and what is prohibited given the scenario. Or you might be asked to develop a "theory" for the case: when faced with an incomplete set of facts about the case, you must fill in the picture based on what is implied by the facts that are known. The problem could be elaborated by the addition of new information or hypotheticals.

No formal training in logic is required to answer these questions correctly. Analytical Reasoning questions are intended to be answered using knowledge, skills, and reasoning ability generally expected of college students and graduates.

Suggested Approach

Some people may prefer to answer first those questions about a passage that seem less difficult and then those that seem more difficult. In general, it is best to finish one passage before starting on another, because much time can be lost in returning to a passage and reestablishing familiarity with its relationships. However, if you are having great difficulty on one particular set of questions and are spending too much time on them, it may be to your advantage to skip that set of questions and go on to the next passage, returning to the problematic set of questions after you have finished the other questions in the section.

Do not assume that because the conditions for a set of questions look long or complicated, the questions based on those conditions will be especially difficult.

Read the passage carefully. Careful reading and analysis are necessary to determine the exact nature of the relationships involved in an Analytical Reasoning passage. Some relationships are fixed (for example, P and R must always work on the same project). Other relationships are variable (for example, Q must be assigned to either team 1 or team 3). Some relationships that are not stated explicitly in the conditions are implied by and can be deduced from those that are stated (for example, if one condition about paintings in a display specifies that Painting K must be to the left of Painting Y, and another specifies that Painting W must be to the left of Painting K, then it can be deduced that Painting W must be to the left of Painting Y).

In reading the conditions, do not introduce unwarranted assumptions. For instance, in a set of questions establishing relationships of height and weight among the members of a team, do not assume that a person who is taller than another person must weigh more than that person. As another example, suppose a set involves ordering and a question in the set asks what must be true if both X and Y must be earlier than Z; in this case, do not assume that X must be earlier than Y merely because X is mentioned before Y. All the information needed to answer each question is provided in the passage and the question itself.

The conditions are designed to be as clear as possible. Do not interpret the conditions as if they were intended to trick you. For example, if a question asks how many people could be eligible to serve on a committee, consider only those people named in the passage unless directed otherwise. When in doubt, read the conditions in their most obvious sense. Remember, however, that the language in the conditions is intended to be read for precise meaning. It is essential to pay particular attention to words that describe or limit relationships, such as "only," "exactly," "never," "always," "must be," "cannot be," and the like.

The result of this careful reading will be a clear picture of the structure of the relationships involved, including the kinds of relationships permitted, the participants in the relationships, and the range of possible actions or attributes for these participants.

Keep in mind question independence. Each question should be considered separately from the other questions in its set. No information, except what is given in the original conditions, should be carried over from one question to another.

In some cases a question will simply ask for conclusions to be drawn from the conditions as originally given. Some questions may, however, add information to the original conditions or temporarily suspend or replace one of the original conditions for the purpose of that question only. For example, if Question 1 adds the supposition "if P is sitting at table 2 ...," this supposition should NOT be carried over to any other question in the set.

Consider highlighting text and using diagrams. Many people find it useful to underline key points in the passage and in each question. In addition, it may prove very helpful to draw a diagram to assist you in finding the solution to the problem.

In preparing for the test, you may wish to experiment with different types of diagrams. For a scheduling problem, a simple calendar-like diagram may be helpful. For a grouping problem, an array of labeled columns or rows may be useful.

Even though most people find diagrams to be very helpful, some people seldom use them, and for some individual questions no one will need a diagram. There is by no means universal agreement on which kind of diagram is best for which problem or in which cases a diagram is most useful. Do not be concerned if a particular problem in the test seems to be best approached without the use of a diagram.

Logical Reasoning Questions

Arguments are a fundamental part of the law, and analyzing arguments is a key element of legal analysis. Training in the law builds on a foundation of basic reasoning skills. Law students must draw on the skills of analyzing, evaluating, constructing, and refuting arguments. They need to be able to identify what information is relevant to an issue or argument and what impact further evidence might have. They need to be able to reconcile opposing positions and use arguments to persuade others.

Logical Reasoning questions evaluate the ability to analyze, critically evaluate, and complete arguments as they occur in ordinary language. The questions are based on short arguments drawn from a wide variety of sources, including newspapers, general interest magazines, scholarly publications, advertisements, and informal discourse. These arguments mirror legal reasoning in the types of arguments presented and in their complexity, though few of the arguments actually have law as a subject matter.

Each Logical Reasoning question requires you to read and comprehend a short passage, then answer one question (or, rarely, two questions) about it. The questions are designed to assess a wide range of skills involved in thinking critically, with an emphasis on skills that are central to legal reasoning.

These skills include:

- Recognizing the parts of an argument and their relationships

- Recognizing similarities and differences between patterns of reasoning

- Drawing well-supported conclusions

- Reasoning by analogy

- Recognizing misunderstandings or points of disagreement

- Determining how additional evidence affects an argument

- Detecting assumptions made by particular arguments

- Identifying and applying principles or rules

- Identifying flaws in arguments

- Identifying explanations

The questions do not presuppose specialized knowledge of logical terminology. For example, you will not be expected to know the meaning of specialized terms such as "ad hominem" or "syllogism." On the other hand, you will be expected to understand and critique the reasoning contained in arguments. This requires that you possess a university-level understanding of widely used concepts such as argument, premise, assumption, and conclusion.

Suggested Approach

Read each question carefully. Make sure that you understand the meaning of each part of the question. Make sure that you understand the meaning of each answer choice and the ways in which it may or may not relate to the question posed.

Do not pick a response simply because it is a true statement. Although true, it may not answer the question posed.

Answer each question on the basis of the information that is given, even if you do not agree with it. Work within the context provided by the passage. LSAT questions do not involve any tricks or hidden meanings.

Reading Comprehension Questions

Both law school and the practice of law revolve around extensive reading of highly varied, dense, argumentative, and expository texts (for example, cases, codes, contracts, briefs, decisions, evidence). This reading must be exacting, distinguishing precisely what is said from what is not said. It involves comparison, analysis, synthesis, and application (for example, of principles and rules). It involves drawing appropriate inferences and applying ideas and arguments to new contexts. Law school reading also requires the ability to grasp unfamiliar subject matter and the ability to penetrate difficult and challenging material.

The purpose of LSAT Reading Comprehension questions is to measure the ability to read, with understanding and insight, examples of lengthy and complex materials similar to those commonly encountered in law school. The Reading Comprehension section of the LSAT contains four sets of reading questions, each set consisting of a selection of reading material followed by five to eight questions. The reading selection in three of the four sets consists of a single reading passage; the other set contains two related shorter passages. Sets with two passages are a variant of Reading Comprehension called Comparative Reading, which was introduced in June 2007.

Comparative Reading questions concern the relationships between the two passages, such as those of generalization/instance, principle/application, or point/counterpoint. Law school work often requires reading two or more texts in conjunction with each other and understanding their relationships. For example, a law student may read a trial court decision together with an appellate court decision that overturns it, or identify the fact pattern from a hypothetical suit together with the potentially controlling case law.

Reading selections for LSAT Reading Comprehension questions are drawn from a wide range of subjects in the humanities, the social sciences, the biological and physical sciences, and areas related to the law. Generally, the selections are densely written, use high-level vocabulary, and contain sophisticated argument or complex rhetorical structure (for example, multiple points of view). Reading Comprehension questions require you to read carefully and accurately, to determine the relationships among the various parts of the reading selection, and to draw reasonable inferences from the material in the selection. The questions may ask about the following characteristics of a passage or pair of passages:

- The main idea or primary purpose

- Information that is explicitly stated

- Information or ideas that can be inferred

- The meaning or purpose of words or phrases as used in context

- The organization or structure

- The application of information in the selection to a new context

- Principles that function in the selection

- Analogies to claims or arguments in the selection

- An author's attitude as revealed in the tone of a passage or the language used

- The impact of new information on claims or arguments in the selection

Suggested Approach

Since reading selections are drawn from many different disciplines and sources, you should not be discouraged if you encounter material with which you are not familiar. It is important to remember that questions are to be answered exclusively on the basis of the information provided in the selection. There is no particular knowledge that you are expected to bring to the test, and you should not make inferences based on any prior knowledge of a subject that you may have. You may, however, wish to defer working on a set of questions that seems particularly difficult or unfamiliar until after you have dealt with sets you find easier.

Strategies. One question that often arises in connection with Reading Comprehension has to do with the most effective and efficient order in which to read the selections and questions. Possible approaches include:

- reading the selection very closely and then answering the questions;

- reading the questions first, reading the selection closely, and then returning to the questions; or

- skimming the selection and questions very quickly, then rereading the selection closely and answering the questions.

Test takers are different, and the best strategy for one might not be the best strategy for another. In preparing for the test, therefore, you might want to experiment with the different strategies and decide what works most effectively for you.

Remember that your strategy must be effective under timed conditions. For this reason, the first strategy— reading the selection very closely and then answering the questions—may be the most effective for you. Nonetheless, if you believe that one of the other strategies

might be more effective for you, you should try it out and assess your performance using it.

Reading the selection. Whatever strategy you choose, you should give the passage or pair of passages at least one careful reading before answering the questions. Try to distinguish main ideas from supporting ideas, and opinions or attitudes from factual, objective information. Note transitions from one idea to the next and identify the relationships among the different ideas or parts of a passage, or between the two passages in Comparative Reading sets. Consider how and why an author makes points and draws conclusions. Be sensitive to implications of what the passages say.

You may find it helpful to mark key parts of passages. For example, you might underline main ideas or important arguments, and you might circle transitional words— "although," "nevertheless," "correspondingly," and the like—that will help you map the structure of a passage. Also, you might note descriptive words that will help you identify an author's attitude toward a particular idea or person.

Answering the Questions

- Always read all the answer choices before selecting the best answer. The best answer choice is the one that most accurately and completely answers the question being posed.

- Respond to the specific question being asked. Do not pick an answer choice simply because it is a true statement. For example, picking a true statement might yield an incorrect answer to a question in which you are asked to identify an author's position on an issue, since you are not being asked to evaluate the truth of the author's position but only to correctly identify what that position is.

- Answer the questions only on the basis of the information provided in the selection. Your own views, interpretations, or opinions, and those you have heard from others, may sometimes conflict with those expressed in a reading selection; however, you are expected to work within the context provided by the reading selection. You should not expect to agree with everything you encounter in Reading Comprehension passages.

THE WRITING SAMPLE

On the day of the test, you will be asked to write one sample essay. LSAC does not score the writing sample, but copies are sent to all law schools to which you apply. According to a 2015 LSAC survey of 129 United States and Canadian law schools, almost all utilize the writing sample in evaluating some applications for admission. Failure to respond to writing sample prompts and frivolous responses have been used by law schools as grounds for rejection of applications for admission.

In developing and implementing the writing sample portion of the LSAT, LSAC has operated on the following premises: First, law schools and the legal profession value highly the ability to communicate effectively in writing. Second, it is important to encourage potential law students to develop effective writing skills. Third, a sample of an applicant's writing, produced under controlled conditions, is a potentially useful indication of that person's writing ability. Fourth, the writing sample can serve as an independent check on other writing submitted by applicants as part of the admission process. Finally, writing samples may be useful for diagnostic purposes related to improving a candidate's writing.

The writing prompt presents a decision problem. You are asked to make a choice between two positions or courses of action. Both of the choices are defensible, and you are given criteria and facts on which to base your decision. There is no "right" or "wrong" position to take on the topic, so the quality of each test taker's response is a function not of which choice is made, but of how well or poorly the choice is supported and how well or poorly the other choice is criticized.

The LSAT writing prompt was designed and validated by legal education professionals. Since it involves writing based on fact sets and criteria, the writing sample gives applicants the opportunity to demonstrate the type of argumentative writing that is required in law school, although the topics are usually nonlegal.

You will have 35 minutes in which to plan and write an essay on the topic you receive. Read the topic and the accompanying directions carefully. You will probably find it best to spend a few minutes considering the topic and organizing your thoughts before you begin writing. In your essay, be sure to develop your ideas fully, leaving time, if possible, to review what you have written. Do not write on a topic other than the one specified. Writing on a topic of your own choice is not acceptable.

No special knowledge is required or expected for this writing exercise. Law schools are interested in the reasoning, clarity, organization, language usage, and writing mechanics displayed in your essay. How well you write is more important than how much you write. Confine your essay to the blocked, lined area on the front and back of the separate Writing Sample Response Sheet. Only that area will be reproduced for law schools. Be sure that your writing is legible.

TAKING THE PREPTEST UNDER SIMULATED LSAT CONDITIONS

One important way to prepare for the LSAT is to simulate the day of the test by taking a practice test under actual time constraints. Taking a practice test under timed conditions helps you to estimate the amount of time you can afford to spend on each question in a section and to determine the question types on which you may need additional practice.

Since the LSAT is a timed test, it is important to use your allotted time wisely. During the test, you may work only on the section designated by the test supervisor. You cannot devote extra time to a difficult section and make up that time on a section you find easier. In pacing yourself, and checking your answers, you should think of each section of the test as a separate minitest.

Be sure that you answer every question on the test. When you do not know the correct answer to a question, first eliminate the responses that you know are incorrect, then make your best guess among the remaining choices. Do not be afraid to guess as there is no penalty for incorrect answers.

When you take a practice test, abide by all the requirements specified in the directions and keep strictly within the specified time limits. Work without a rest period. When you take an actual test, you will have only a short break—usually 10–15 minutes—after SECTION III.

When taken under conditions as much like actual testing conditions as possible, a practice test provides very useful preparation for taking the LSAT.

Official directions for the four multiple-choice sections and the writing sample are included in this PrepTest so that you can approximate actual testing conditions as you practice.

To take the test:

- Set a timer for 35 minutes. Answer all the questions in SECTION I of this PrepTest. Stop working on that section when the 35 minutes have elapsed.

- Repeat, allowing yourself 35 minutes each for sections II, III, and IV.

- Set the timer again for 35 minutes, then prepare your response to the writing sample topic at the end of this PrepTest.

- Refer to "Computing Your Score" for the PrepTest for instruction on evaluating your performance. An answer key is provided for that purpose.

The practice test that follows consists of four sections corresponding to the four scored sections of the December 2017 LSAT. Also reprinted is the December 2017 unscored writing sample topic.

General Directions for the LSAT Answer Sheet

e actual testing time for this portion of the test will be 2 hours 55 minutes. There are five sections, each with a time limit of 35 nutes. The supervisor will tell you when to begin and end each section. If you finish a section before time is called, you may check ur work on that section **only;** do not turn to any other section of the test book and do not work on any other section either in the test ok or on the answer sheet.

ere are several different types of questions on the test, and each question type has its own directions. **Be sure you understand the ections for each question type before attempting to answer any questions in that section.**

t everyone will finish all the questions in the time allowed. Do not hurry, but work steadily and as quickly as you can without crificing accuracy. You are advised to use your time effectively. If a question seems too difficult, go on to the next one and return to e difficult question after completing the section. **MARK THE BEST ANSWER YOU CAN FOR EVERY QUESTION. NO DEDUCTIONS LL BE MADE FOR WRONG ANSWERS. YOUR SCORE WILL BE BASED ONLY ON THE NUMBER OF QUESTIONS YOU JSWER CORRECTLY.**

L YOUR ANSWERS MUST BE MARKED ON THE ANSWER SHEET. Answer spaces for each question are lettered to correspond h the letters of the potential answers to each question in the test book. After you have decided which of the answers is correct, cken the corresponding space on the answer sheet. **BE SURE THAT EACH MARK IS BLACK AND COMPLETELY FILLS THE JSWER SPACE.** Give only one answer to each question. If you change an answer, be sure that all previous marks are **erased mpletely.** Since the answer sheet is machine scored, incomplete erasures may be interpreted as intended answers. **ANSWERS :CORDED IN THE TEST BOOK WILL NOT BE SCORED.**

ere may be more question numbers on this answer sheet than there are questions in a section. Do not be concerned, but be certain t the section and number of the question you are answering matches the answer sheet section and question number. Additional swer spaces in any answer sheet section should be left blank. Begin your next section in the number one answer space for that ction.

AC takes various steps to ensure that answer sheets are returned from test centers in a timely manner for processing. In the unlikely ent that an answer sheet is not received, LSAC will permit the examinee either to retest at no additional fee or to receive a refund of or her LSAT fee. **THESE REMEDIES ARE THE ONLY REMEDIES AVAILABLE IN THE UNLIKELY EVENT THAT AN ANSWER IEET IS NOT RECEIVED BY LSAC.**

Score Cancellation

omplete this section only if you are bsolutely certain you want to cancel our score. **A CANCELLATION :EQUEST CANNOT BE RESCINDED. YOU ARE AT ALL UNCERTAIN, OU SHOULD NOT COMPLETE THIS ECTION.**

o cancel your score from this dministration, you **must:**

. fill in both ovals here ...... ○ ○
          AND

. read the following statement. Then sign your name and enter the date. **YOUR SIGNATURE ALONE IS NOT SUFFICIENT FOR SCORE CANCELLATION. BOTH OVALS ABOVE MUST BE FILLED IN FOR SCANNING EQUIPMENT TO RECOGNIZE YOUR REQUEST FOR SCORE CANCELLATION.**

certify that I wish to cancel my test core from this administration. I nderstand that my request is reversible and that my score will ot be sent to me or to the law chools to which I apply.

_____
ign your name in full

_____
ate

FOR LSAC USE ONLY   ●

HOW DID YOU PREPARE FOR THE LSAT?
(Select all that apply.)

Responses to this item are voluntary and will be used for statistical research purposes only.

○ By studying the free sample questions available on LSAC's website.
○ By taking the free sample LSAT available on LSAC's website.
○ By working through official LSAT *PrepTests*, *ItemWise*, and/or other LSAC test prep products.
○ By using LSAT prep books or software **not** published by LSAC.
○ By attending a commercial test preparation or coaching course.
○ By attending a test preparation or coaching course offered through an undergraduate institution.
○ Self study.
○ Other preparation.
○ No preparation.

CERTIFYING STATEMENT

Please write the following statement. Sign and date.

I certify that I am the examinee whose name appears on this answer sheet and that I am here to take the LSAT for the sole purpose of being considered for admission to law school. I further certify that I will neither assist nor receive assistance from any other candidate, and I agree not to copy, retain, or transmit examination questions in any form or discuss them with any other person.

_____
_____
_____
_____
_____
_____
_____
_____
_____

SIGNATURE: _____ TODAY'S DATE: ____ / ____ / ____
                                                              MONTH DAY YEAR

SCANTRON® EliteView™ EM-295665-1:654321

INSTRUCTIONS FOR COMPLETING THE BIOGRAPHICAL AREA ARE ON THE BACK COVER OF YOUR TEST BOOKLET.
USE ONLY A NO. 2 OR HB PENCIL TO COMPLETE THIS ANSWER SHEET. DO NOT USE INK.

1 LAST NAME · FIRST NAME · MI

2 LAST 4 DIGITS OF SOCIAL SECURITY/ SOCIAL INSURANCE NO.

3 LSAC ACCOUNT NUMBER

4 CENT NUMBE

5 DATE OF BIRTH — MONTH DAY YEAR
Jan, Feb, Mar, Apr, May, June, July, Aug, Sept, Oct, Nov, Dec

6 TEST FORM CODE

7 RACIAL/ETH DESCRIPTI
Mark one or
1 Amer. Indian/Alas
2 Asian
3 Black/African Ar
4 Canadian Aborig
5 Caucasian/Whit
6 Hispanic/Latino
7 Native Hawaiian
   Other Pacific Isl
8 Puerto Rican
9 TSI/Aboriginal A

8 SEX
Male
Female

9 DOMINANT LANGUAGE
English
Other

10 ENGLISH FLUENCY
Yes
No

11 TEST DATE
MONTH DAY YEAR

12 TEST FORM

Law School Admission Test

Mark one and only one answer to each question. Be sure to fill in completely the space for your intended answer choice. If you erase, do so completely. Make no stray marks.

SECTION 1, SECTION 2, SECTION 3, SECTION 4, SECTION 5 (questions 1–30, choices A B C D E)

13 TEST BOOK SERIAL NO.

14 PLEASE PRINT INFORMAT
LAST NAME
FIRST NAME
DATE OF BIRTH

THE PREPTEST

SECTION I

Time—35 minutes

25 Questions

Directions: Each question in this section is based on the reasoning presented in a brief passage. In answering the questions, you should not make assumptions that are by commonsense standards implausible, superfluous, or incompatible with the passage. For some questions, more than one of the choices could conceivably answer the question. However, you are to choose the best answer; that is, choose the response that most accurately and completely answers the question and mark that response on your answer sheet.

1. The mayoral race in Bensburg is a choice between Chu, a prodevelopment candidate, and Lewis, who favors placing greater limits on development. Prodevelopment candidates have won in the last six mayoral elections. Thus, Chu will probably defeat Lewis.

Which one of the following statements, if true, most weakens the argument?

(A) Lewis has extensive experience in national politics, but not in city politics.
(B) Prodevelopment mayoral candidates in Bensburg generally attract more financial backing for their campaigns.
(C) Bensburg is facing serious new problems that most voters attribute to overdevelopment.
(D) Lewis once worked as an aide to a prodevelopment mayor of Bensburg.
(E) Chu was not thought of as a prodevelopment politician before this election.

2. Rose: Let's not see the movie *Winter Fields*. I caught a review of it in the local paper and it was the worst review I've read in years.

Chester: I don't understand why that might make you not want to see the movie. And besides, nothing in that paper is particularly well written.

Chester's response suggests that he misinterpreted which one of the following expressions used by Rose?

(A) see the movie
(B) caught a review
(C) local paper
(D) worst review
(E) in years

3. Enrique: The city's transit authority does not have enough money to operate for the next twelve months without cutting service or increasing fares, and the federal government has so far failed to provide additional funding. Nonetheless, the transit authority should continue operating without service cuts or fare increases until it has exhausted its funds. At that point, the federal government will be willing to provide funding to save the authority.

Cynthia: If the transit authority tries that maneuver, the federal government will probably just let the authority go out of business. The transit authority cannot risk allowing that to happen.

The dialogue most strongly supports the claim that Enrique and Cynthia disagree over whether

(A) the transit authority should continue operating without cutting service or increasing fares until it has exhausted its funds
(B) the federal government should provide additional funding to the transit authority
(C) it would be better for the transit authority to cut services than it would be to raise fares
(D) the federal government is willing to provide additional funding to the transit authority now
(E) the transit authority can afford to operate for the next twelve months without cutting service even if it does not receive additional funding

GO ON TO THE NEXT PAGE.

4. A survey published in a leading medical journal in the early 1970s found that the more frequently people engaged in aerobic exercise, the lower their risk of lung disease tended to be. Since other surveys have confirmed these results, it must be the case that aerobic exercise has a significant beneficial effect on people's health.

The reasoning above is questionable because the argument

(A) ignores anecdotal evidence and bases its conclusion entirely on scientific research

(B) considers only surveys published in one particular medical journal

(C) concludes merely from the fact that two things are correlated that one causes the other

(D) presumes, without providing justification, that anyone who does not have lung disease is in good health

(E) fails to consider that even infrequent aerobic exercise may have some beneficial effect on people's health

5. Researchers examined 100 people suffering from herniated disks in their backs. Five of them were found to have a defect in a particular gene. The researchers also examined 100 people who had no problems with the disks in their backs; none had the genetic defect. They concluded that the genetic defect increases the likelihood of herniated disks.

Which one of the following, if true, most strengthens the researchers' reasoning?

(A) The researchers also examined a group of 100 people who did not have the defective gene; 80 were found to have herniated disks in their backs.

(B) When the researchers examined a group of 100 people with the defective gene, they found that 2 of them had herniated disks in their backs.

(C) When the researchers examined the families of the 5 subjects who had the defective gene, they found that 30 family members also had the defective gene, and each of them suffered from herniated disks.

(D) Another team of researchers examined a different group of 100 people who suffered from herniated disks, and they found that none of them had the defective gene.

(E) When the researchers examined the family of one of the subjects who did not suffer from herniated disks, they found 30 family members who did not have the defective gene, and 20 of them suffered from herniated disks.

6. The only vehicles that have high resale values are those that are well maintained. Thus any well-maintained vehicle has a high resale value.

The flawed nature of the argument can most effectively be demonstrated by noting that, by parallel reasoning, we could argue that

(A) since none of the plants in this garden have been pruned before, no plant in this garden needs pruning

(B) since the best mediators have the longest track records, the worst mediators have the shortest track records

(C) since only those who desire to become astronauts actually become astronauts, that desire must be the most important factor involved in determining who will become an astronaut

(D) since all city dwellers prefer waterfalls to traffic jams, anyone who prefers waterfalls to traffic jams is a city dweller

(E) since one's need for medical care decreases as one's health improves, a person who is in an excellent state of health has no need of medical care

7. Rita: No matter how you look at them, your survey results are misleading. Since people generally lie on such surveys, the numbers you collected are serious underestimates.

Hiro: I have no doubt that people lie on surveys of this type. The question is whether some people lie more than others. While the raw numbers surely underestimate what I'm trying to measure, the relative rates those numbers represent are probably close to being accurate.

Rita and Hiro disagree over whether

(A) the survey results are misleading regardless of how they are interpreted

(B) people tend to lie on certain kinds of surveys

(C) a different type of measure than a survey would produce results that are less misleading

(D) the raw numbers collected are serious underestimates

(E) the number of people surveyed was adequate for the survey's purpose

GO ON TO THE NEXT PAGE.

8. Lopez: Our university is not committed to liberal arts, as evidenced by its decision to close the classics department. The study of classical antiquity is crucial to the liberal arts, and it has been so since the Renaissance.

   Warrington: Although the study of classical works is essential to the liberal arts, a classics department isn't, since other departments often engage in that study.

   Warrington's argument proceeds by

   (A) offering additional reasons in favor of the conclusion of Lopez's argument
   (B) claiming that the reasoning in Lopez's argument rests on an illicit appeal to tradition
   (C) mounting a direct challenge to the conclusion of Lopez's argument
   (D) responding to a possible objection to the reasoning in Lopez's argument
   (E) presenting a consideration in order to undermine the reasoning in Lopez's argument

9. Ted, a senior employee, believes he is underpaid and attempts to compensate by routinely keeping short hours, though it is obvious to everyone that he still makes some valuable, unique, and perhaps irreplaceable contributions. Tatiana, Ted's supervisor, is aware of the deficit in Ted's performance, and realizes other workers work harder than they should to make up for it. Nevertheless, Tatiana decides that she should not request that Ted be replaced.

   Which one of the following principles, if valid, would most help to justify Tatiana's decision?

   (A) Supervisors should request that an employee be replaced only if they know that all the work done by that employee can be performed equally well by another employee.
   (B) Employers should compensate all their employees in a way that is adequate in relation to the value of the contributions they make.
   (C) Only someone with greater authority than a particular employee's supervisor is entitled to decide whether that employee should be replaced.
   (D) Workers in a work setting should regard themselves as jointly responsible for the work to be performed.
   (E) An employee's contributions in the workplace are not always a function of the amount of time spent on the job.

10. One adaptation that enables an animal species to survive despite predation by other species is effective camouflage. Yet some prey species with few or no other adaptations to counteract predation have endured for a long time with black-and-white coloration that seems unlikely to provide effective camouflage.

    Which one of the following, if true, most contributes to a resolution of the apparent discrepancy mentioned above?

    (A) Most species with black-and-white coloration are more populous than the species that prey upon them.
    (B) No form of camouflage is completely effective against all kinds of predators.
    (C) Animals of many predatory species do not perceive color or pattern in the same manner as humans do.
    (D) Conspicuous black-and-white areas help animals of the same species avoid encounters with one another.
    (E) Black-and-white coloration is not as great a liability against predators at night as it is during the day.

11. Lecturer: If I say, "I tried to get my work done on time," the meanings of my words do not indicate that I didn't get it done on time. But usually you would correctly understand me to be saying that I didn't. After all, if I had gotten my work done on time, I would instead just say, "I got my work done on time." And this example is typical of how conversation works.

    The lecturer's statements, if true, most strongly support which one of the following statements?

    (A) Understanding what people say often requires more than just understanding the meanings of the words they use.
    (B) It is unusual for English words to function in communication in the way that "tried" does.
    (C) Understanding what people use a word to mean often requires detecting their nonverbal cues.
    (D) Speakers often convey more information in conversation than they intend to convey.
    (E) Listeners cannot reasonably be expected to have the knowledge typically required for successful communication.

GO ON TO THE NEXT PAGE.

12. Legislator: The recently passed highway bill is clearly very unpopular with voters. After all, polls predict that the majority party, which supported the bill's passage, will lose more than a dozen seats in the upcoming election.

The reasoning in the legislator's argument is most vulnerable to criticism on the grounds that the argument

(A) gives no reason to think that the predicted election outcome would be different if the majority party had not supported the bill

(B) focuses on the popularity of the bill to the exclusion of its merit

(C) infers that the bill is unpopular from a claim that presupposes its unpopularity

(D) takes for granted that the bill is unpopular just because the legislator wishes it to be unpopular

(E) bases its conclusion on the views of voters without establishing their relevant expertise on the issues involved

13. Songwriters get much of the money they earn from their songs from radio airplay. A hit song is played thousands of times, and the songwriter is paid for each play. Only a fraction of songwriters actually achieve a hit, however, and even fewer manage to write several. Writers of hit songs are often asked to write songs for movie sound tracks, but they sometimes decline, because although such songs frequently become hits, their writers receive single up-front payments rather than continued revenues from radio airplay.

If the statements above are true, which one of the following must be true?

(A) Any songwriter who receives revenue from radio airplay has written a hit song.

(B) All songwriters who write songs for movie sound tracks have had their songs played on the radio thousands of times.

(C) Some songs written for movie sound tracks are played on the radio thousands of times.

(D) Most songwriters prefer the possibility of continued income to single up-front payments for their songs.

(E) Some songwriters earn money solely from the radio airplay of their songs.

14. Debate coach: Britta's command of the historical facts was better than Robert's, and that led to the distinct impression that Britta won the debate. But it's also important to evaluate how reasonable the debaters' arguments were, regardless of their ability to bring the facts to bear in those arguments. When you take that into consideration, Robert's debate performance was as good as Britta's.

The debate coach's argument depends on the assumption that

(A) Britta's arguments were quite unreasonable

(B) Robert's arguments were more reasonable than Britta's

(C) good debate performances require very reasonable arguments

(D) neither Britta nor Robert was in full command of the facts

(E) winning a debate requires having a good command of the facts

GO ON TO THE NEXT PAGE.

15. Physicists attempting to create new kinds of atoms often do so by fusing together two existing atoms. For such fusion to occur, the two atoms must collide with enough energy—that is, at high enough speeds—to overcome the electromagnetic force by which atoms repel each other. But if the energy with which two atoms collide greatly exceeds the minimum required for the fusion to take place, the excess energy will be converted into heat, making the resulting new atom very hot. And the hotter the atom is, the greater the chance that it will immediately split apart again.

Which one of the following is most strongly supported by the information above?

(A) When physicists create new kinds of atoms by fusing together two existing atoms, the new atoms usually split apart again immediately.

(B) If a new atom produced by the collision of two other atoms immediately splits apart again, then the collision did not produce enough energy to overcome the electromagnetic force by which atoms repel each other.

(C) The stronger the electromagnetic force by which two atoms repel each other, the hotter any new atom will be that is created by the fusion of those two atoms.

(D) Whenever two existing atoms are made to collide and fuse together into a new atom, little energy is produced in the collision unless the new atom immediately splits apart.

(E) If two atoms collide with considerably more energy than is needed for fusion to take place, the new atom will be likely to immediately split apart again.

16. Fremont: Simpson is not a viable candidate for chief executive of Pod Oil because he has no background in the oil industry.

Galindo: I disagree. An oil industry background is no guarantee of success. Look no further than Pod Oil's last chief executive, who had decades of oil industry experience but steered the company to the brink of bankruptcy.

Galindo's argument is flawed in that it

(A) fails to justify its presumption that Fremont's objection is based on personal bias

(B) fails to distinguish between relevant experience and irrelevant experience

(C) rests on a confusion between whether an attribute is necessary for success and whether that attribute is sufficient for success

(D) bases a conclusion that an attribute is always irrelevant to success on evidence that it is sometimes irrelevant to success

(E) presents only one instance of a phenomenon as the basis for a broad generalization about that phenomenon

17. Discharges of lightning from a volcanic ash cloud occur only when the cloud's highest point exceeds an altitude of 5 kilometers. Those discharges become progressively more frequent as the ash cloud moves higher still. Weather radar can measure the altitude of ash clouds, but it is not available in all parts of the world. Hence lightning discharge data can sometimes be our only reliable indicator of the altitude of ash clouds.

Which one of the following is an assumption required by the argument?

(A) The highest point of any volcanic ash cloud will eventually exceed an altitude of 5 kilometers.

(B) Lightning discharges can be detected in some regions in which weather radar is unavailable.

(C) Weather radar is no less accurate in determining the altitude of volcanic ash clouds than it is in determining the altitude of regular clouds.

(D) A volcanic ash cloud whose highest point exceeds an altitude of 5 kilometers is likely to be at least partly beyond the reach of weather radar.

(E) Lightning discharges are no more frequent for large volcanic ash clouds than for small volcanic ash clouds.

GO ON TO THE NEXT PAGE.

18. If the standards committee has a quorum, then the general assembly will begin at 6:00 P.M. today. If the awards committee has a quorum, then the general assembly will begin at 7:00 P.M. today.

Which one of the following statements follows logically from the statements above?

(A) If the general assembly does not begin at 6:00 P.M. today, then the awards committee has a quorum.

(B) If the standards committee does not have a quorum, then the awards committee has a quorum.

(C) If the general assembly begins at 6:00 P.M. today, then the standards committee has a quorum.

(D) If the general assembly does not begin at 7:00 P.M. today, then the standards committee has a quorum.

(E) If the standards committee has a quorum, then the awards committee does not have a quorum.

19. One of the things lenders do in evaluating the risk of a potential borrower defaulting on a loan is to consider the potential borrower's credit score. In general, the higher the credit score, the less the risk of default. Yet for mortgage loans, the proportion of defaults is much higher for borrowers with the highest credit scores than for other borrowers.

Which one of the following, if true, most helps to resolve the apparent discrepancy in the statements above?

(A) Mortgage lenders are much less likely to consider risk factors other than credit score when evaluating borrowers with the highest credit scores.

(B) Credit scores reported to mortgage lenders are based on collections of data that sometimes include errors or omit relevant information.

(C) A potential borrower's credit score is based in part on the potential borrower's past history in paying off debts in full and on time.

(D) For most consumers, a mortgage is a much larger loan than any other loan the consumer obtains.

(E) Most potential borrowers have credit scores that are neither very low nor very high.

20. Computer modeling of reasoning tasks is far easier than computer modeling of other cognitive tasks, such as the processing of sense images. Computers can defeat chess champions, but cannot see. So, it appears that we understand the analytical capabilities of our minds much better than we understand our senses.

Which one of the following principles, if valid, most helps to justify the reasoning above?

(A) The degree of difficulty of constructing computer models of cognitive tasks is a good index of the degree of difficulty of performing those tasks.

(B) The better we understand a computer's ability to perform a type of task, the better we will understand our own ability to perform it.

(C) A computer's defeat of a chess champion should count as an indication that the computer possesses true intelligence.

(D) The less difficult it is to construct a computer model of a process the better understood is that process.

(E) We should not underestimate the usefulness of computer modeling to the study of human cognition.

21. Archaeologist: Our team discovered 5,000-year-old copper tools near a Canadian river, in a spot that offered easy access to the raw materials for birchbark canoes—birch, cedar, and spruce trees. The tools are of a sort used by the region's Aboriginal people in making birchbark canoes in more recent times. It is likely therefore that Aboriginal people in Canada built birchbark canoes 5,000 years ago.

The archaeologist's argument depends on the assumption that the copper tools that were found

(A) had no trade value 5,000 years ago

(B) were present in the region 5,000 years ago

(C) were designed to be used on material from birch, cedar, and spruce trees only

(D) were the only kind of tool that would have been used for canoe making 5,000 years ago

(E) are not known to have been used by the region's Aboriginal people for any task other than canoe making

GO ON TO THE NEXT PAGE.

22. Advertisement: Hypnosis videos work to alter behavior by subliminally directing the subconscious to act in certain ways. Directions to the subconscious must, however, be repeated many times in order to be effective. Hypnosis videos from Mesmosis, Inc. induce a hypnotic state and then issue an initial command to the subject's subconscious to experience each subsequent instruction as if it had been repeated 1,000 times. Because of the initial instruction, the subsequent instructions on Mesmosis videos are extremely effective—it is as if they had actually been repeated 1,000 times!

The advertisement's reasoning is most vulnerable to criticism on the grounds that the advertisement

(A) overlooks a requirement that it states for the effectiveness of directions to the subconscious

(B) takes for granted that the effectiveness of a direction to the subconscious is always directly proportional to the number of times the direction is repeated

(C) concludes that hypnosis is the most effective technique for altering behavior without considering evidence supporting other techniques

(D) draws a conclusion that simply restates a claim presented in support of that conclusion

(E) concludes that hypnosis videos will be effective simply because they have never been proven to be ineffective

23. The traditional view of the Roman emperor Caligula as a cruel and insane tyrant has been challenged by some modern historians. They point out that little documentation of Caligula's alleged cruelty or outrageous behavior survives from the time of his reign and that the histories that have come down to us were written by his enemies.

Which one of the following, if true, adds the most support for the challenge from the modern historians?

(A) There is less documentation of any sort from Caligula's reign than from the reigns of most other Roman emperors of Caligula's era.

(B) People who have lived under someone regarded as a cruel tyrant are more likely to view that person unfavorably than favorably.

(C) The specific outrageous acts attributed to Caligula in Roman documentation are very similar to acts attributed in earlier writings to other rulers alleged to be cruel tyrants.

(D) The little documentation that survives from Caligula's reign indicates that the Roman people believed Caligula to be crueler than other emperors who were widely thought to be tyrants.

(E) There is ample documentation of modern tyrants being responsible for outrageous acts worse than those attributed to Caligula.

GO ON TO THE NEXT PAGE.

24. Critics of a plan to create new building sites from land that currently lies under only 5 meters of water claim that it will reduce the habitat area available to a local subpopulation of dolphins. It is true that the dolphins never enter water more than 30 meters deep, and the current area of habitation is bounded on one side by land and everywhere else by water that is considerably deeper than that. Nevertheless, the critics are mistaken, because _____.

Which one of the following most logically completes the argument?

(A) the dolphins' current habitat area is large enough to support a dolphin population several times the size of the current one
(B) the dolphins do not inhabit water that is less than 10 meters deep
(C) the most serious threat to the dolphin subpopulation is not habitat reduction but disease and ocean pollution
(D) the average depth of water in the dolphins' habitat area is 25 meters
(E) a short distance from the dolphins' habitat area, the ocean floor drops to a depth of 100 meters

25. Any popular television series that is groundbreaking is critically acclaimed. But not all popular television series are critically acclaimed. Thus, not all popular television series are groundbreaking.

The pattern of reasoning in the argument above is most similar to that in which one of the following arguments?

(A) If articles use specialized technical terminology, they are not widely read. So, since all academic works use specialized technical terminology, articles are not widely read if they are academic works.
(B) Professor Attah gives students high grades if she thinks their work is greatly improved. So, since she gives some of her students high grades, she thinks those students' work is greatly improved.
(C) If a biography is unbiased, it contains embarrassing facts about its subject. So, since not all biographies contain embarrassing facts about their subjects, not all biographies are unbiased.
(D) Mr. Schwartz is polite to anyone who is polite to him. So, since all of his colleagues are polite to him, it must be that he is polite to all his colleagues.
(E) If a book is worth reading, it is worth buying. So, since not all books are worth reading, not all books are worth buying.

S T O P
IF YOU FINISH BEFORE TIME IS CALLED, YOU MAY CHECK YOUR WORK ON THIS SECTION ONLY.
DO NOT WORK ON ANY OTHER SECTION IN THE TEST.

SECTION II

Time—35 minutes

27 Questions

<u>Directions</u>: Each set of questions in this section is based on a single passage or a pair of passages. The questions are to be answered on the basis of what is <u>stated</u> or <u>implied</u> in the passage or pair of passages. For some questions, more than one of the choices could conceivably answer the question. However, you are to choose the <u>best</u> answer; that is, choose the response that most accurately and completely answers the question and mark that response on your answer sheet.

The following passage is adapted from an article published in 1981.

Chinese is a language of many distinct dialects that are often mutually unintelligible. Some linguists have argued that a new dialect of Chinese has evolved in the United States, which is commonly used in the
(5) Chinatown section of San Francisco. The characterization of this "Chinatown Chinese" as a distinct dialect is based primarily on two claims: first, that it is so different from any other dialect used in China that a person newly arrived from that country might have a
(10) difficult time communicating with a Chinese American in San Francisco who speaks nominally the same language as the newcomer, and, second, that no matter which of the traditional Chinese dialects one speaks, one can communicate effectively with other Chinese
(15) Americans in San Francisco so long as one is proficient in the uniquely Chinese-American terminologies.

Regarding the first claim, much of the distinctive vocabulary of Chinatown Chinese consists of proper names of geographical places and terms for things
(20) that some people, especially those born and raised in villages, had never encountered in China. Some are transliterated terms, such as *dang-tang* for "downtown." Others are direct translations from American English, such as *gong-ngihn ngiht* ("labor" plus "day") for
(25) "Labor Day." However, the core of the language brought to the U.S. by Chinese people has remained intact. Thus, the new vocabulary has supplemented, but not supplanted, the traditional language in the traditional dialects. In fact, normal conversations can
(30) be conducted fairly readily between Chinese-speaking Chinese Americans and new arrivals from China, provided that they speak the same traditional Chinese dialect as each other. Terms not familiar to the newcomer, most of which would name objects, places,
(35) and events that are part of the local experience, can easily be avoided or explained by the speaker, or their meaning can be inferred from the context. The supposed language barrier is, therefore, mostly imaginary.

The second claim—that the sharing of a uniquely
(40) Chinese-American vocabulary makes possible communication among Chinese Americans no matter what their basic dialect of Chinese may be—is a misleading oversimplification. While many Chinese-American speakers of other Chinese dialects
(45) have become familiar with Cantonese, now the most common dialect of Chinese spoken in the U.S., through watching Cantonese movies and by hearing that dialect in Hong Kong, Guandong, or the U.S., this is not the same thing as sharing a single unique

(50) dialect. Moreover, the dialects of Chinese can differ markedly in their systems of sounds and, to some extent, in grammar and vocabulary, and these differences persist among Chinese-American speakers of these various dialects. Hence, even a common
(55) vocabulary for such things as names of U.S. cities, street names, and non-Chinese items does not guarantee mutual intelligibility because these words constitute only a minute percentage of each dialect and are generally peripheral to the core vocabulary.

1. Which one of the following most accurately expresses the main point of the passage?

(A) Linguists who argue that Chinatown Chinese constitutes a distinct new dialect are mistaken because it is intelligible to speakers of the Cantonese dialect.

(B) Because Chinatown Chinese is unfamiliar to many native Chinese people, linguists have concluded that it constitutes a distinct new dialect of Chinese.

(C) The primary claims supporting the view that Chinatown Chinese is a distinct new dialect do not stand up to close examination.

(D) Because visitors from China can fairly easily converse with Chinese Americans living in San Francisco, the variety of language there cannot be designated a distinct new dialect.

(E) Although Chinese dialects are difficult to define with certainty, linguists are now in agreement that Chinatown Chinese does not constitute a distinct new dialect.

2. The passage suggests that a visitor from China who speaks the same traditional dialect as a Chinese-American person in San Francisco would find it most difficult to converse with that person about

(A) news from China
(B) mutual relatives in San Francisco
(C) the Chinese American's daily life in the U.S.
(D) the Chinese visitor's feelings about the U.S.
(E) Chinese cultural traditions

GO ON TO THE NEXT PAGE.

3. The author mentions the words *dang-tang* (line 22) and *gong-ngihn ngiht* (line 24) in order to

(A)   demonstrate the extent to which American English terms dominate Chinatown Chinese

(B)   illustrate how Chinese Americans are able to communicate with each other easily despite using different dialects

(C)   explain why native Chinese are able to understand Chinese Americans with relative ease

(D)   show why Chinatown Chinese should be considered a distinct new dialect

(E)   exemplify the ways in which American English terms have become part of or have influenced Chinatown Chinese

4. According to the passage, in San Francisco the traditional Chinese dialects spoken by Chinese immigrants to the U.S.

(A)   remain at their core essentially the same over time

(B)   eventually merge with other Chinese dialects

(C)   undergo subtle changes in sound and grammatical structure

(D)   are often abandoned by native speakers for the Cantonese dialect

(E)   lose much of their traditional vocabulary as they incorporate transliterated American English terms

5. When the passage refers to "transliterated terms" (line 22), the author most likely means words

(A)   whose sounds and meanings have been directly incorporated into another language

(B)   that name objects, places, and events that are part of local experience

(C)   that are written in the same way in another language

(D)   that are direct translations from another language

(E)   that sound different in different dialects

GO ON TO THE NEXT PAGE.

In a typical Hollywood action movie, the hero skirts death to complete a mission. Bad guys shoot, cars explode, objects fall from the sky, but all just miss. If any one of those things happened just a little
(5) differently, the hero would be dead. Yet the hero survives.

In some respects, the story of our universe resembles an action movie. A slight change to any one of the laws of physics would likely have caused some disaster that would have disrupted the normal
(10) evolution of the universe and made life impossible. For example, if the strong nuclear force had been slightly stronger or weaker, stars would have forged very little of the carbon that seems necessary to form planets and living things. Indeed, it seems that in order
(15) for a universe to support life, the laws of physics must be so finely tuned that the very existence of such a universe becomes improbable.

Some cosmologists have tried to reconcile the existence of our universe with the seeming
(20) improbability of its existence by hypothesizing that our universe is but one of many universes within a wider array called the multiverse. In almost all of those universes, the laws of physics might not allow the formation of matter as we know it and therefore
(25) of life. But given the sheer number of possibilities, nature would have had a good chance to get the "right" set of laws at least once.

But just how exceptional is the set of physical laws governing our universe? The view that the laws
(30) of physics are finely tuned arises largely from the difficulty scientists have had in identifying alternative sets of laws that would be compatible with life.

The conventional way scientists explore whether a particular constant of physics is finely tuned is to
(35) tweak it while leaving all other constants unaltered. The scientists then "play the movie" of that universe— they do calculations, what-if scenarios, or computer simulations—to see what disasters occur. But there is no reason to tweak just one parameter at a time. By
(40) manipulating multiple constants at once, my colleague and I have identified numerous scenarios—hypothetical universes—where the physical laws would be very different from our own and yet compatible with the formation of complex structures and perhaps even
(45) some forms of intelligent life.

Fine tuning has been invoked by some cosmologists as indirect evidence for the multiverse. Do our findings therefore call the concept of the multiverse into question? I do not think this is necessarily the case for
(50) two reasons. First, certain models of the birth of the universe would lead us to expect the existence of something like the multiverse. Secondly, the multiverse concept may well prove to be the source of solutions to certain other long-standing puzzles in cosmology.

6. Which one of the following most accurately states the main point of the passage?

(A) Although the universe seems finely tuned for the existence of life, there may be more sets of physical laws that would be compatible with life than commonly thought.

(B) Although the multiverse hypothesis was developed to explain the apparent fine tuning of the physical laws of our universe, it may be useful for explaining other kinds of issues in cosmology.

(C) When scientists have tried modeling hypothetical universes by altering physical laws, they have been unable to find alternate sets of laws that are consistent with life.

(D) The improbability of life occurring in the universe supports the idea that our universe is just one of many universes in a broader multiverse.

(E) The story of our universe resembles an action movie in that, despite all of the circumstances that could have had disastrous consequences for the emergence of life, life exists.

7. It can be inferred from the passage that when the author says that scientists "play the movie" (second sentence of the fifth paragraph), the author means that they

(A) acknowledge the fictional nature of what is being described

(B) follow a theoretical chain of events to its conclusion

(C) highlight how dramatic the situation is that follows

(D) model their work on certain common archetypes

(E) play an active role in shaping the story

8. The passage suggests that the cosmologists mentioned in the third paragraph would be most likely to agree with which one of the following statements?

(A) Our universe is affected by what occurs in other universes.

(B) The existence of multiple universes makes each universe more likely to contain life.

(C) The laws of physics must be the same in every part of the multiverse.

(D) There are enough universes to make it probable that life exists in at least one of them.

(E) There is only one universe in the multiverse that contains life.

GO ON TO THE NEXT PAGE.

9. The author would be most likely to agree with which one of the following statements about the conventional way in which scientists investigate the apparent fine tuning of physical laws?

    (A)   It focuses on looking for outcomes that are irrelevant to the issue at hand.
    (B)   It is too unfocused to produce useful results.
    (C)   It has been conducted without concern for mathematical rigor.
    (D)   Its methodology results in an overly restricted set of outcomes.
    (E)   It will eventually produce a workable model of an alternate universe with life.

10. The final paragraph of the passage functions primarily to

    (A)   demonstrate the inadequacy of the view that the author is arguing against
    (B)   indicate the kinds of questions to which the author's research can be extended
    (C)   discuss the implications of the author's research
    (D)   consider two potential counterarguments to the author's position
    (E)   suggest a course of future experimentation to test the author's conclusions

11. The author's attitude toward the multiverse hypothesis can best be described as one of

    (A)   dismissiveness
    (B)   skepticism
    (C)   open-mindedness
    (D)   advocacy
    (E)   enthusiasm

12. If the multiverse hypothesis as discussed in the third paragraph is correct, then the story of the hero in the first paragraph would be more analogous to the story of our universe if the hero

    (A)   had a team of supporters working behind the scenes to make sure that the hero succeeded
    (B)   was actually just one of many people sent on the mission, but almost all of the others failed
    (C)   had developed the survival skills needed to complete the mission during a series of previous missions
    (D)   was actually just one of many people sent on the mission, and each person found a unique way to succeed
    (E)   was equipped with a map that made it possible to know where each danger lurked and how to avoid it

GO ON TO THE NEXT PAGE.

Passage A

Comedians are not amused when their jokes are stolen, and for that reason we might expect joke-stealing disputes to ripen into lawsuits occasionally. Copyright is the most relevant body of law; formally, it applies to
(5) jokes and comedic routines. Yet copyright infringement lawsuits between rival comedians are all but unheard of, despite what appears to be a persistent practice of joke stealing among stand-up comedians. The nonexistence of such lawsuits is a product of both
(10) practical considerations that render the cost of enforcing the formal law prohibitively expensive, and legal hurdles that make success difficult and uncertain in lawsuits relating to joke stealing. In the end, copyright law simply does not provide comedians with a
(15) cost-effective way of protecting their comedic material.

Conventional intellectual property wisdom holds that absent formal legal protection, there would be scant production of creative works, as potential creators would be deterred by the unlikelihood of
(20) recouping the cost of their creations. If there is no effective legal protection against joke theft, then why do thousands of comedians keep cranking out new material night after night?

The answer to this question is that, in stand-up
(25) comedy, social norms substitute for intellectual property law. Taken as a whole, this norms system governs a wide array of issues that generally parallel those ordered by copyright law. These norms are not merely hortatory. They are enforced with sanctions,
(30) including simple badmouthing and refusals to work with an offending comedian. These sanctions, while extralegal, can cause serious reputational harm to an alleged joke thief, and may substantially hamper a comedian's career. Using this informal system,
(35) comedians are able to assert ownership of jokes, regulate their use and transfer, impose sanctions on transgressors, and maintain substantial incentives to invest in new material.

Passage B

Accomplished chefs consider their recipes to be
(40) a very valuable form of intellectual property. At the same time, recipes are *not* a form of innovation that is effectively covered by current intellectual property laws. Recipes are rarely patentable, and combinations of ingredients cannot be copyrighted. Legal protections
(45) are potentially available via trade secrecy laws, but chefs very seldom use them. Instead, three implicit social norms are operative among chefs, and together these norms function in a manner quite similar to law-based intellectual property systems.
(50) First, a chef must not copy another chef's recipe innovation exactly. The function of this norm is analogous to patenting in that the community acknowledges the right of a recipe inventor to exclude others from practicing his or her invention, even if all
(55) the information required to do so is publicly available. A second norm mandates that, if a chef reveals recipe-related secret information to a colleague, that colleague must not pass the information on to others without permission. This norm gives a chef a property

(60) right similar to that attainable via a contract under trade secrecy law. A third norm is that colleagues must credit developers of significant recipes as the authors of that information. This norm operates in a manner analogous to copyright protection.

13. Both passages are primarily concerned with investigating which one of the following topics?

(A) the legal protections available to creators of intellectual property

(B) the connection between the enforcement of social norms and the incentives these norms provide to creators of intellectual property

(C) the extent to which the rights of creators of intellectual property must be balanced against the social value of making that property publicly available

(D) the practical considerations that prompt creators of intellectual property to forgo legal protections of their work

(E) the ways in which social norms can take the place of laws in protecting intellectual property

14. Passage A, but not passage B, discusses

(A) the relationship of social norms to intellectual property laws

(B) the evolution of social norms

(C) the enforcement of social norms

(D) the limitations of social norms

(E) the impact of social norms on creative output

15. Which one of the following questions is addressed by passage A but not by passage B with respect to the group of professionals discussed?

(A) How can members of the group share their creative work with colleagues without sacrificing their intellectual property rights?

(B) Why do members of the group usually choose not to make use of the legal protections that are potentially available to them?

(C) To what extent can patent law protect the creative output of members of the group?

(D) What is a form of creative output that members of the group regard as intellectual property?

(E) What social norms prohibit members of the group from violating the intellectual property rights of other members of the group?

GO ON TO THE NEXT PAGE.

16. The author of passage A would be most likely to agree with which one of the following statements?

    (A) Comedians rarely acknowledge the degree to which their own comedic material is influenced by the work of their peers.
    (B) Comedians would be more likely to protect their comedic material through copyright law if they had greater assurance that they could successfully bring infringement lawsuits against perceived perpetrators of joke theft.
    (C) Creative rights to jokes and comedic routines should be protected by trade secrecy law rather than by copyright law.
    (D) The system of social norms operative among comedians is not robust enough to allow comedians to be properly compensated for the expenses they incur when developing new comedic material.
    (E) In the particular context of stand-up comedy, no informal system for protecting intellectual property can be as effective as a formal system.

17. Which one of the following statements is most strongly supported by information given in the passages?

    (A) Intellectual property violations are more frequent among comedians than among chefs.
    (B) A more elaborate system of social norms has developed among chefs than among comedians.
    (C) Chefs enjoy more significant legal protections of their intellectual property than do comedians.
    (D) Most comedians and chefs are satisfied with current intellectual property laws.
    (E) Comedians and chefs both derive some professional benefit from observing the social norms of their profession.

18. The relationship described in passage A as holding between comedians and copyright law is most analogous to the relationship described in passage B as holding between chefs and which one of the following?

    (A) intellectual property
    (B) patent law
    (C) the combinations of ingredients in a recipe
    (D) trade secrecy law
    (E) social norms

19. The author of passage A would be most likely to agree with which one of the following statements?

    (A) The social norms that are operative among comedians make it possible for individual comedians to recoup the costs associated with developing a comedic routine.
    (B) Comedians should increase their reliance on copyright law as a means of protecting their comedic routines.
    (C) Most professional comedians are largely unconcerned with the expense involved in developing new comedic material.
    (D) Law-based intellectual property systems generally work less efficiently than systems based on social norms.
    (E) Existing copyright law should be modified to make it more cost effective for comedians to protect their comedic material through legal means.

20. Which one of the following, if true, would most clearly support the argument made in passage B?

    (A) There is no social norm preventing chefs from using colleagues' recipes as inspiration, as long as those recipes are not copied exactly.
    (B) Chefs are significantly more likely to deny requested information to colleagues whom they believe have violated the operative social norms.
    (C) Recipes published in cookbooks are protected by copyright law from being published in other cookbooks.
    (D) The community of chefs is too small to effectively enforce sanctions against those who violate the operative social norms.
    (E) In practice it is virtually impossible to determine whether a chef has copied a colleague's recipe exactly or has instead independently developed that recipe.

GO ON TO THE NEXT PAGE.

The novelist and social theorist Charlotte Perkins Gilman, whose writings were widely read and discussed in the early twentieth century, played an important role in the debate about the theories of
(5) Charles Darwin and their application to society. Darwin's theory of evolution did not directly apply to social ideology, but various intellectuals translated his ideas of natural selection into social language and argued about their interpretation. Some of these
(10) Social Darwinist theorists held that the nature of human social interactions is strictly determined by the process of biological evolution, and that it is futile to try to meddle with the competitive struggle for existence and the survival of the fittest. Another, more
(15) activist group of Social Darwinists held that although changes in human societies, like those that occur in biological species, do constitute a sort of evolution, this evolution at the level of a human society need not be competitive, but can emerge through collective
(20) action within society.

Gilman identified herself with this latter ideological camp and applied evolutionary theory in the movement for social change. The central thesis of this group of Social Darwinists was that although
(25) people, like all life, are the products of natural evolutionary forces, the principles of change that determine the development of organisms have brought humans to the point where it is possible for us to contribute consciously to the evolutionary process, to
(30) redesign and mold our societies in appropriate ways. This, for Gilman, was not simply a descriptive observation about humanity but was also a source of ethical responsibility. She argued that since a prime source of social evolution is human work, whether in
(35) crafts, trades, arts, or sciences, one of the primary ethical responsibilities of a person is to identify and engage in work that is societally relevant and that makes the best use of that person's talents.

Gilman was not merely engaged in an intellectual
(40) debate. Motivated by her ethical vision and convinced of the plasticity of human nature, Gilman vehemently sought to break the molds into which people, especially women, had been thrust. In both her fiction and her social theory she urges women to further social
(45) evolution by collectively working toward a reorganization of society. A central goal of the reorganization she envisioned would be the abandonment of gender-specific work roles and hierarchical relationships. Gilman believed that at one time such
(50) arrangements had been necessary for evolution because what she felt were male traits of assertiveness, combat, and display were essential for the development of a complex society. Future progress, she believed, now required the restoration of a balance that would
(55) include what she saw as female qualities of cooperation and nurturance.

21. Which one of the following most accurately expresses the main point of the passage?

(A) Gilman's activist social theory, which called for the abolition of gender-specific work roles, contributed the central doctrine to one type of Social Darwinism that distinguished it from the other, more competitive-minded Social Darwinist camp.

(B) Although Gilman aligned herself with the activist group of Social Darwinists, she rejected some of its doctrines, calling instead for gender equality and the general recognition of traditionally female qualities.

(C) Unlike most Social Darwinists of her time, Gilman saw the issues involved in Social Darwinist debate as transcending abstract theoretical concerns and having important implications for human society, especially for women.

(D) Gilman's version of Social Darwinism held that people can and should contribute actively to the social evolution of humanity, and in her writings she advised women to do so through efforts to eliminate traditional gender roles.

(E) Gilman, whose important contributions to the debate over the application of Darwinism to social ideology were widely recognized in the early twentieth century, should also be recognized for her writings on women's social issues.

22. The passage most strongly suggests that which one of the following statements is true?

(A) Gilman's social theory was unlike other applications of evolutionary theory to the social realm because it was not closely allied with any of the major political movements of her time.

(B) One of Gilman's innovations was the introduction of social discourse into the debate about the theories of Charles Darwin, which prior to her work had focused purely on biological issues.

(C) Gilman worked in direct collaboration with other social activists toward the implementation of a set of social reforms that were based on her evolutionary doctrines.

(D) Charles Darwin's writings on the evolution of biological species influenced Gilman's work only indirectly through the writings of other Social Darwinists.

(E) Other evolutionary theorists contemporary with or prior to Gilman shared her view about whether or not evolutionary theory has implications for social practice.

GO ON TO THE NEXT PAGE.

23. Which one of the following sequences most accurately expresses the organization of the passage?

    (A) The author identifies a particular individual as a proponent of one of two versions of a theory, and then describes how that individual drew practical implications from the theory and relates some of those implications.
    (B) The author describes the relationship of a particular individual to an intellectual community, characterizes in general terms a theory held by that individual, contrasts that theory with another related theory, and then rejects one of those two competing theories.
    (C) The author proposes an interpretation of a particular individual's writings, explains how those writings relate to a more general theoretical context, and then argues for the proposed interpretation of the individual's writings.
    (D) The author describes some reasoning used by a group of theorists, evaluates that reasoning, attributes similar reasoning to a particular individual, and then shows how the proposed evaluation applies to specific arguments made by that individual.
    (E) The author presents some historical facts about the development of a scientific theory, explains the role played by a particular individual in the formulation of that theory, and then summarizes the responses of critics to that individual's work.

24. The passage indicates that Gilman believed that which one of the following can be a significant factor in the evolution of society?

    (A) reclamation of ancient social theories
    (B) cross-cultural communication
    (C) greater literacy
    (D) skilled occupations
    (E) future uses of dialectical methods in the social sciences

25. The passage gives evidence that Gilman valued which one of the following as an instrument of social progress in her time?

    (A) industrialization
    (B) fiction writing
    (C) international travel
    (D) religious training
    (E) combative personality traits

26. The passage can most accurately be described as which one of the following?

    (A) a defense of the principles of social theory that were promulgated by a particular group of writers and activists
    (B) a description of the role played by a particular writer in an intellectual controversy over the consequences of a scientific theory
    (C) an explication of the theoretical points of disagreement between two closely related social theories that have almost identical goals
    (D) a defense of one interpretation of a particular writer's views, together with a rejection of a competing interpretation of those views
    (E) an introduction to a general type of scientific theory, clarified by a detailed presentation of one writer's version of that theory

27. Which one of the following is implied by Gilman's views as described in the passage?

    (A) Some social conditions on which social evolution depends at certain times in human history are detrimental to further social evolution at other times in history.
    (B) The types of changes that constitute genuine social evolution can no longer be brought about except through coordinated efforts directed at consciously formulated goals.
    (C) Gender-based hierarchical relationships, which predated, and led to the development of, gender-specific work roles, will probably be especially difficult to eradicate.
    (D) While Social Darwinist theories are essentially descriptive and thus do not have ethical implications, they can be useful rhetorically in communicating ethical messages.
    (E) Continuation of the process of social evolution will lead inevitably to the inclusion of more cooperation and nurturance in social arrangements.

S T O P

IF YOU FINISH BEFORE TIME IS CALLED, YOU MAY CHECK YOUR WORK ON THIS SECTION ONLY.
DO NOT WORK ON ANY OTHER SECTION IN THE TEST.

SECTION III

Time—35 minutes

26 Questions

Directions: Each question in this section is based on the reasoning presented in a brief passage. In answering the questions, you should not make assumptions that are by commonsense standards implausible, superfluous, or incompatible with the passage. For some questions, more than one of the choices could conceivably answer the question. However, you are to choose the best answer; that is, choose the response that most accurately and completely answers the question and mark that response on your answer sheet.

1. Advertisement: Most nutritionists recommend eating fish twice a week. Eating tilapia fillets is a perfect choice for those who want the benefits of eating fish but do not care for the taste of fish. Tilapia fillets lack the strong fishy taste that many people find objectionable.

   Which one of the following, if true, most seriously weakens the advertisement's argument?

   (A) Eating more than the recommended amount of fish can cause toxins that are present in high concentrations in many varieties of fish to accumulate in a person's body.
   (B) Tilapia are invasive species that crowd out native species of fish in lakes throughout the world.
   (C) Tilapia fillets contain little of the beneficial fish oils that are the main reason nutritionists recommend eating fish frequently.
   (D) Most people who do not care for the taste of fish eat less fish than is recommended by most nutritionists.
   (E) People who rarely or never eat fish usually dislike any food with a strong fishy taste.

2. Domestication of animals is a cooperative activity, and cooperative activities require a sophisticated means of communication. Language provides just such a means. It is likely, therefore, that language developed primarily to facilitate animal domestication.

   A flaw in the argument is that the argument

   (A) conflates being necessary for the development of a phenomenon with guaranteeing the development of that phenomenon
   (B) takes for granted that every phenomenon has a unique cause
   (C) infers that the development of one phenomenon caused the development of another merely because the two phenomena developed around the same time
   (D) draws a conclusion that merely restates a claim presented in support of that conclusion
   (E) assumes that if something serves a purpose it must have developed in order to serve that purpose

3. Many employers treat their employees fairly. Thus, using others as a means to one's own ends is not always morally reprehensible or harmful to others.

   The argument requires the assumption that

   (A) some employers act in a morally reprehensible manner only when they harm those whom they employ
   (B) no employers who act morally use their employees as a means to their own ends
   (C) some or all employers use their employees as a means to their own ends
   (D) making a profit from the labor of others is personally advantageous but never harmful
   (E) it is not possible to harm someone else without treating that person as a means to one's own ends

4. Editorial: It is common to find essays offering arguments that seem to show that our nation is in decline. There is no cause for alarm, however. The anxious tone of these essays shows that the problem is with the psychological state of their writers rather than with the actual condition of our nation.

   Which one of the following most accurately describes a flaw in the editorial's reasoning?

   (A) The editorial dismisses a claim without considering any reasons presented in arguments for that claim.
   (B) The editorial compares two situations without considering the obvious differences between them.
   (C) The editorial confuses claims about a cultural decline with claims about a political decline.
   (D) The editorial overlooks the possibility that the nation is neither thriving nor in decline.
   (E) The editorial dismisses a particular view while offering evidence that actually supports that view.

GO ON TO THE NEXT PAGE.

5. Eating turmeric, a spice commonly found in curries, probably helps prevent Alzheimer's disease. More turmeric is consumed per capita in India than in the rest of the world, and the incidence of Alzheimer's disease is much lower there than it is worldwide. Furthermore, Alzheimer's disease is characterized by the buildup of amyloid protein plaques in the brain, and studies on animals found that curcumin—a compound found in turmeric—reduces the accumulation of amyloid proteins.

Which one of the following, if true, most strengthens the argument?

(A) Rosemary and ginger, which contain compounds that affect amyloid protein accumulation much like curcumin does, are commonly found in the diets of people living in India.

(B) Many scientists believe that the buildup of amyloid protein plaques in the brain is a symptom of Alzheimer's disease rather than a cause.

(C) The proportion of people living in India who fall within the age group that is most prone to developing Alzheimer's disease is smaller than the proportion of people worldwide who fall within that age group.

(D) None of the other compounds found in turmeric have been studied to see whether they affect the accumulation of amyloid proteins.

(E) The parts of India that have the highest per capita rates of curry consumption have the lowest incidence of Alzheimer's disease.

6. Forestry official: Many people think that if forest fires are not extinguished as quickly as possible, the Forestry Department is not doing its job properly. But relatively frequent, small fires clear out small trees and forest debris, which, if allowed to accumulate, would create the conditions for large, devastating fires. Therefore, it's best to let small fires burn.

The statement that relatively frequent, small fires clear out small trees and forest debris plays which one of the following roles in the official's argument?

(A) It is offered as support for the contention that the Forestry Department is not doing its job properly if it does not extinguish forest fires as quickly as possible.

(B) It is used as evidence against the contention that the Forestry Department is not doing its job properly if it does not extinguish forest fires as quickly as possible.

(C) It is used to show what the consequences would be if the Forestry Department based its policies on the ideas most people have about how it should do its job.

(D) It is an example used to illustrate the claim that most people believe the Forestry Department should quickly extinguish all forest fires.

(E) It is a conclusion based on the premise in the argument that it is best to let small forest fires burn.

7. Gerald: Unless a consumer secures his or her home wireless Internet service, anyone strolling by is able to access that person's service with certain laptop computers or smartphones. Such use cannot be considered illegal under current laws: it's no more like trespassing than is enjoying music playing on someone's radio as you walk down the street.

Kendra: But unlike hearing music while walking by, accessing wireless service requires stopping for a considerable length of time. And that could be considered loitering or even harassment.

Gerald's and Kendra's positions indicate that they disagree over whether accessing someone's wireless Internet service while walking down the street

(A) can be considered illegal under current law
(B) is like trespassing
(C) should be prohibited by law
(D) requires a considerable length of time
(E) could be done without intending to do so

GO ON TO THE NEXT PAGE.

8. Over the last thousand years, plant species native to islands have gone extinct at a much faster rate than have those native to mainland regions. Biologists believe that this is because island plants have not adapted the defenses against being eaten by large land mammals that mainland plants have. Ordinarily, populations of large land mammals are not established on islands until after the island is colonized by humans.

Which one of the following, if true, most strongly supports the biologist's explanation cited above?

(A) Most of the plant species in the world that have not yet gone extinct are native to mainland regions.

(B) Many plant species that are not native to islands have become very well established on islands throughout the world.

(C) Commercial development on many islands has resulted in loss of habitat for many native plants.

(D) The rate of extinction of native plant species on an island tends to increase dramatically after human colonization.

(E) Large land mammals tend to prefer plants from species native to mainland regions over plants from species native to islands.

9. As regards memory, the brain responds best to repeated patterns, such as the melodic and rhythmic patterns of music. This is why we can remember long strings of information or text, which would normally be impossible to memorize, when they are put to music. Given that music aids memory, it might seem that funny jokes would be easy to remember, since, like music, they normally elicit an emotional response in us. However, jokes are usually very difficult to remember, since _____.

Which one of the following most logically completes the passage?

(A) jokes, unlike music, always have content that is verbal or at least clearly symbolic

(B) some successful jokes are short and pithy, whereas others are long and involved

(C) jokes work not by conforming to repeated patterns but by breaking them

(D) for most people, certain memories elicit a strong emotional response

(E) people can hold in short-term memory only a few chunks of unpatterned information at a time

10. The prehistoric fish Tiktaalik is the earliest known animal with fingers. Since variations were so great among prehistoric fish species, Tiktaalik would not have stood out as unusual at the time. However, Tiktaalik's fingers were an important development in animal evolution because it is likely that Tiktaalik is an ancestor to the many land animals with fingers.

The statements above, if true, most strongly support which one of the following?

(A) Tiktaalik likely used its fingers to move on land.

(B) Tiktaalik's fingers were its only feature to play a significant role in the development of modern land animals.

(C) Tiktaalik is not the ancestor of any currently surviving fish species.

(D) No fish without fingers would ever be able to move on land.

(E) The evolutionary significance of Tiktaalik could not be determined just through comparison to fish species of its time.

11. Gabriella: By raising interest rates, the government has induced people to borrow less money and therefore to spend less, thereby slowing the country's economy.

Ivan: I disagree with your analysis. The country's economy is tied to the global economy. Whatever happens to the global economy also happens here, and the global economy has slowed. Therefore, the government's action did not cause the economy's slowdown.

Gabriella and Ivan disagree about whether

(A) the economic slowdown in the country has caused people to spend less

(B) the economy of the country is tied to the economies of other countries

(C) raising interest rates caused a significant decrease in borrowing

(D) raising interest rates caused the country's economy to slow

(E) the global economy has slowed

GO ON TO THE NEXT PAGE.

12. In a scene in an ancient Greek play, *Knights*, the character Demosthenes opens a writing tablet on which an oracle had written a prophecy, and while looking at the tablet, he continuously expresses his amazement at its contents. His companion presses him for information, whereupon Demosthenes explains what the oracle had written.

Of the following claims, which one can most justifiably be rejected on the basis of the statements above?

(A) In ancient Greek plays, characters are presumed to know how to read unless their illiteracy is specifically mentioned.
(B) The character of Demosthenes in *Knights* is not based on a historical figure.
(C) In ancient Greek plays, the reading aloud of written texts commonly occurred as part of the on-stage action.
(D) In ancient Greece, people did not read silently to themselves.
(E) Only rarely in ancient Greece were prophecies written down on writing tablets.

13. Science cannot adequately explain emotional phenomena such as feeling frustrated, falling in love, or being moved by a painting. Since they cannot be explained by physics, chemistry, or neurophysiology, human emotions must not be physical phenomena.

The conclusion follows logically if which one of the following is assumed?

(A) Whatever is not a physical phenomenon cannot be explained by science.
(B) Nothing that can be felt by only one subject can be studied scientifically.
(C) Physics, chemistry, and neurophysiology have similar explanatory frameworks.
(D) Whatever is not a physical phenomenon is an emotional one.
(E) Every physical phenomenon can be explained by physics, chemistry, or neurophysiology.

14. Several *Tyrannosaurus rex* skeletons found in North America contain tooth marks that only a large carnivore could have made. At the time *T. rex* lived, it was the only large carnivore in North America. The tooth marks could have resulted only from combat or feeding. But such tooth marks would have been almost impossible to inflict on the skeleton of a live animal.

The information above most strongly supports which one of the following?

(A) *T. rex* regularly engaged in combat with smaller carnivores.
(B) At the time *T. rex* lived, it was common for carnivores to feed on other carnivores.
(C) *T. rex* sometimes engaged in cannibalism.
(D) *T. rex* sometimes engaged in intraspecies combat.
(E) At the time *T. rex* lived, there were large carnivores on continents other than North America.

15. There is a popular view among literary critics that a poem can never be accurately paraphrased because a poem is itself the only accurate expression of its meaning. But these same critics hold that their own paraphrases of particular poems are accurate. Thus, their view that poetry cannot be accurately paraphrased is false.

The reasoning in the argument is most vulnerable to the criticism that the argument

(A) presupposes the falsity of the view that it sets out to refute
(B) takes for granted that the main purpose of poems is to convey information rather than express feelings
(C) takes for granted that a paraphrase of a poem cannot be useful to its readers unless it accurately expresses a poem's meaning
(D) provides no justification for favoring one of the literary critics' beliefs over the other
(E) provides no justification for following one particular definition of "paraphrase"

GO ON TO THE NEXT PAGE.

16. The tax bill passed 2 years ago provides substantial incentives for businesses that move to this area and hire 50 or more employees. Critics say the bill reduces the government's tax revenues. Yet clearly it has already created many jobs in this area. Last year, Plastonica qualified for incentives under the bill by opening a new plastics factory here that hired 75 employees.

The argument's reasoning depends on which one of the following assumptions?

(A) If Plastonica had not opened the plastics factory in the area, it would not have opened a plastics factory at all.

(B) Plastonica would not have opened the plastics factory in the area had it not been for the incentives.

(C) Most critics of the tax bill claim that it will not create any more new jobs.

(D) If Plastonica had not opened the plastics factory in the area, it would have opened it somewhere else.

(E) Critics of the tax bill believe that it has not created any jobs in the area.

17. When a chain of service stations began applying a surcharge of $0.25 per purchase on fuel paid for by credit card, the chain's owners found that this policy made their customers angry. So they decided instead to simply raise the price of fuel a compensatory amount and give a $0.25 discount to customers paying with cash. Customers were much happier with this policy.

Which one of the following generalizations does the situation described above most clearly illustrate?

(A) People usually adopt beliefs without carefully assessing the evidence for and against those beliefs.

(B) People's perceptions of the fairness of a policy sometimes depend on whether that policy benefits them personally.

(C) People usually become emotional when considering financial issues.

(D) People often change their minds about issues that do not make significant differences to their lives.

(E) People's evaluations of a situation sometimes depend less on the situation itself than on how it is presented to them.

18. Herbalist: Many herbal medicines work best when they have a chance to influence the body gently over several months. However, many of these herbal medicines have toxic side effects when taken daily for such long periods. Therefore, at least some people who use herbal medicines daily should occasionally skip their usual dose for a day or two, to give the body a chance to recuperate.

Which one of the following is an assumption required by the herbalist's argument?

(A) At least some people who use herbal medicines daily use them for periods long enough for the medicines to have side effects.

(B) At least some herbal medicines work less well in achieving their desired effects if one occasionally skips one's usual dose than if one does not.

(C) Some herbal medicines have toxic side effects when taken for several months, even if the usual dose is occasionally skipped for a day or two to give the body a chance to recuperate.

(D) Anyone who uses herbal medicines should give those medicines a chance to influence the body gently over several months at least.

(E) One should occasionally skip one's usual dose of an herbal medicine for a day or two only if doing so will reduce or eliminate toxic side effects from several months of use.

GO ON TO THE NEXT PAGE.

19. Business owner: Around noon in one section of the city, food trucks that sell lunch directly to customers on the sidewalk occupy many of the limited metered parking spaces available, thus worsening already bad traffic congestion. This led the city council to consider a bill to prohibit food trucks from parking in metered spaces in any commercially zoned area. This bill should be rejected since there is plenty of available parking and little traffic congestion in most areas of the city.

Which one of the following principles, if valid, most helps to justify the business owner's argument?

(A) Unless a business provides a product or service that is valued by consumers, the business should not be allowed to make use of scarce city resources.

(B) If a serious problem exists in one part of a city, the city government should address the problem before it spreads to another area of the city.

(C) No proposed solution to a city problem should be implemented until the problem has been thoroughly studied.

(D) A law that would disadvantage businesses of a certain type throughout a city should not be used to solve a problem that does not affect most areas of the city.

(E) If a city has a serious problem, then it should not implement any policy that would aggravate that problem even if the policy would address another serious problem.

20. Michele: In my professional experience, it's usually not a good idea for a company to overhaul its databases. The rewards rarely exceed the problems experienced along the way, and I'd suggest that anyone considering a database overhaul think twice before proceeding.

Alvaro: But the problems are always caused by a failure to recode the database properly. The best advice for a company considering a database overhaul is to do the job right.

Michele and Alvaro disagree with each other about which one of the following?

(A) why companies should consider overhauling their databases

(B) whether the problems experienced during a database overhaul ever outweigh the rewards

(C) which kinds of database overhauls have more problems than are justified by the rewards

(D) what a company should do when considering a database overhaul

(E) when professional experience is required to correctly recode a database

21. In an experiment, subjects were shown a series of images on a computer screen, appearing usually at the top but occasionally at the bottom. Subjects were asked to guess each time where the next image would appear on the screen. They guessed correctly less than half of the time. The subjects all reported that they based their guesses on patterns they believed they saw in the sequence. Instead, if they had simply guessed that the next image would always appear at the top, they would have been correct most of the time.

If all of the statements above are true, which one of the following must also be true?

(A) If the subjects had always guessed that the next image would appear at the top, they would not have been basing their guesses on any pattern they believed they saw in the sequence.

(B) Basing one's guesses about what will happen next on the basis of patterns one believes one sees is less likely to lead to correct guesses than always guessing that what has happened before will happen next.

(C) There was no predictable pattern that one could reasonably believe occurred in the series of images on the computer screen.

(D) Some of the subjects sometimes guessed that the next image would appear at the bottom of the computer screen, but were incorrect.

(E) The most rational strategy for guessing correctly where the next image would appear would have been simply to always guess that the image would appear at the top.

GO ON TO THE NEXT PAGE.

22. The temperature in Taychester is always at least 10 degrees lower than the temperature in Charlesville. However, the average resident of Charlesville spends 10 to 20 percent more on winter heating expenses than does the average resident of Taychester.

Each of the following, if true, helps to resolve the apparent paradox described above EXCEPT:

(A) Heat loss due to wind is less in Taychester than in Charlesville.

(B) Although Charlesville is always fairly warm during the daytime, temperatures in Charlesville drop steeply at night.

(C) Utility rates in Taychester are lower than utility rates in Charlesville.

(D) People who are used to warmer temperatures generally keep their homes warmer in the winter than do people who are used to colder temperatures.

(E) Houses in colder climates are usually better insulated than houses in warmer climates.

23. Each new car in the lot at Rollway Motors costs more than $18,000. Any car in their lot that is ten or more years old costs less than $5,000. Thus, if a car in Rollway's lot costs between $5,000 and $18,000, it is a used car that is less than ten years old.

The pattern of reasoning in which one of the following arguments is most similar to that in the argument above?

(A) Each apartment above the fourth floor of the building has more than two bedrooms. But all apartments below the fourth floor have fewer than two bedrooms. Thus, any apartment on the fourth floor of the building has exactly two bedrooms.

(B) Each apartment above the fourth floor of the building has two or three bedrooms. But no apartment below the fourth floor has more than two bedrooms. Thus, all of the building's three-bedroom apartments are on the fourth floor or higher.

(C) No apartment above the fourth floor of the building has fewer than three bedrooms. But all apartments below the fourth floor have fewer than two bedrooms. Thus, if there are apartments in the building with exactly two bedrooms, they are on the fourth floor.

(D) No apartment above the fourth floor of the building has more than two bedrooms. But only three-bedroom apartments have balconies. Thus, if any apartment in the building has a balcony, it is on the fourth floor or lower.

(E) Each apartment above the fourth floor of the building has more than two bedrooms. The building has no vacant apartments on or below the fourth floor. Thus, if there is any vacant apartment in the building, it will have more than two bedrooms.

GO ON TO THE NEXT PAGE.

24. Meteorologist: The number of tornadoes reported annually has more than doubled since the 1950s. But their actual number has probably not increased. Our ability to find tornadoes has improved, so we're probably just finding a higher percentage of them than we used to.

Which one of the following, if true, provides the most support for the meteorologist's argument?

(A) The physical damage caused by the average tornado has remained roughly constant since the 1950s.

(B) The number of tornadoes hitting major population centers annually has more than doubled since the 1950s.

(C) The number of large and medium sized tornadoes reported annually has remained roughly constant since the 1950s.

(D) The annual number of deaths due to tornadoes has increased steadily since the 1950s.

(E) The geographic range in which tornadoes are most prevalent has remained roughly constant since the 1950s.

25. Salesperson: If your vacuuming needs are limited to cleaning small areas of uncarpeted floors, an inexpensive handheld vacuum cleaner is likely to be sufficient. After all, most are easy to use and will likely satisfy all your vacuuming needs on wood and tile floors.

The conclusion of the salesperson's argument is most strongly supported if which one of the following is assumed?

(A) The only types of floor surfaces that most consumers encounter are carpet, wood, and tile.

(B) Inexpensive handheld vacuum cleaners are sufficient for cleaning small areas of carpeted floors.

(C) Any handheld vacuum cleaner that is easy to use but sufficient only for cleaning small areas of uncarpeted floors is likely to be inexpensive.

(D) If your household cleaning needs include cleaning small areas of uncarpeted floors, it is likely that you will need a vacuum cleaner.

(E) The more versatile a vacuum cleaner is, the more likely it is to be expensive.

26. Decreased reliance on fossil fuels is required if global warming is to be halted. The current reliance would decrease if economic incentives to develop alternative energy sources were present. So ending global warming requires offering economic incentives to develop alternative energy sources.

The flawed pattern of reasoning exhibited by the argument above most closely parallels that exhibited by which one of the following?

(A) If we end poverty we will end hunger. Ending unemployment will end poverty. So ending unemployment will end hunger.

(B) Daily exercise guarantees good health. Good health ensures a happy life. So daily exercise is required for good health.

(C) Going to college is required for getting a professional job. Graduating from high school is necessary for going to college. So graduating from high school is necessary for getting a professional job.

(D) Keeping good teachers is necessary for improving education. If teachers' salaries were improved, good teachers would remain in the profession. So an increase in teachers' salaries is necessary to improve education.

(E) Preventing abuse of prescription drugs requires expanding drug education efforts. Increased cooperation between schools and law enforcement agencies is needed if drug education efforts are to be expanded. So, if cooperation between law enforcement and schools increases, the abuse of prescription drugs will be prevented.

S T O P
IF YOU FINISH BEFORE TIME IS CALLED, YOU MAY CHECK YOUR WORK ON THIS SECTION ONLY.
DO NOT WORK ON ANY OTHER SECTION IN THE TEST.

SECTION IV

Time—35 minutes

23 Questions

Directions: Each set of questions in this section is based on a scenario with a set of conditions. The questions are to be answered on the basis of what can be logically inferred from the scenario and conditions. For each question, choose the response that most accurately and completely answers the question and mark that response on your answer sheet.

Questions 1–5

A travel agent is arranging a tour made up of visits to exactly four of six cities—Hanoi, Jakarta, Manila, Osaka, Shanghai, and Taipei. Each city that is included in the tour will be visited only once. The tour's schedule is subject to the following constraints:

Hanoi and Taipei must be included in the tour, but they cannot be visited consecutively.

If Osaka is included in the tour, Shanghai cannot be.

If Jakarta is included in the tour, it must be visited third.

If both Jakarta and Manila are included, they must be visited consecutively.

1. Which one of the following could be the tour's schedule, with the four cities included in the tour listed in the order in which they are visited?

(A)   Jakarta, Taipei, Shanghai, Hanoi
(B)   Manila, Taipei, Jakarta, Hanoi
(C)   Osaka, Hanoi, Shanghai, Taipei
(D)   Shanghai, Taipei, Manila, Hanoi
(E)   Taipei, Manila, Jakarta, Shanghai

GO ON TO THE NEXT PAGE.

2. If Shanghai is visited fourth, which one of the following must be true?

   (A) Hanoi is visited second.
   (B) Jakarta is visited third.
   (C) Manila is visited second.
   (D) Osaka is visited second.
   (E) Taipei is visited first.

3. Any of the following could be true EXCEPT:

   (A) Jakarta is visited immediately after Hanoi
        is visited.
   (B) Manila is visited at some time after Jakarta
        is visited.
   (C) Osaka is included in the tour but is not visited
        third.
   (D) Manila is the only city visited between the visits
        to Hanoi and Taipei.
   (E) More than one city is visited between the visits
        to Hanoi and Taipei.

4. If Manila is not included in the tour, which one of the following must be true?

   (A) Hanoi is visited first.
   (B) Jakarta is visited third.
   (C) Osaka is visited second.
   (D) Shanghai is visited third.
   (E) Taipei is visited fourth.

5. If Osaka is visited second, how many of the six cities could be the one visited fourth?

   (A) one
   (B) two
   (C) three
   (D) four
   (E) five

GO ON TO THE NEXT PAGE.

Questions 6–11

A music professor must set the order in which her students will give performances in a concert. Exactly five students will perform—Gloria, Hazel, Roberto, Sonja, and Toshiro. The students will perform one at a time, and each student will perform only once. The following conditions restrict the order in which the students perform:

Hazel must perform earlier than Roberto.

If Gloria performs earlier than Toshiro, then Roberto and Sonja must also perform earlier than Toshiro.

Hazel must perform either earlier than both Sonja and Toshiro or else later than both of them.

6. If Gloria performs first, which one of the following could be true?

(A) Hazel performs third.
(B) Roberto performs second.
(C) Roberto performs fifth.
(D) Sonja performs third.
(E) Toshiro performs fourth.

GO ON TO THE NEXT PAGE.

7. Which one of the following pairs could be the first and second students to perform, respectively?

   (A) Gloria and Toshiro
   (B) Hazel and Gloria
   (C) Roberto and Toshiro
   (D) Sonja and Roberto
   (E) Toshiro and Hazel

8. Which one of the following pairs CANNOT be the fourth and fifth students to perform, respectively?

   (A) Gloria and Toshiro
   (B) Hazel and Roberto
   (C) Roberto and Toshiro
   (D) Sonja and Gloria
   (E) Toshiro and Roberto

9. Which one of the following pairs CANNOT be the second and third students to perform, respectively?

   (A) Gloria and Hazel
   (B) Hazel and Roberto
   (C) Roberto and Toshiro
   (D) Sonja and Gloria
   (E) Toshiro and Sonja

10. If Sonja performs first, which one of the following must be true?

   (A) Gloria performs third.
   (B) Gloria performs fourth.
   (C) Hazel performs third.
   (D) Roberto performs fifth.
   (E) Toshiro performs second.

11. If Sonja performs fifth, which one of the following must be true?

   (A) Gloria performs third.
   (B) Hazel performs first.
   (C) Hazel performs fourth.
   (D) Roberto performs second.
   (E) Toshiro performs second.

GO ON TO THE NEXT PAGE.

Questions 12–17

The operator of a passenger railway system needs to close at least one of its stations. Six stations—L, M, N, P, Q, and R—are being considered for closure. The decision regarding which stations to close and which to keep open is subject to the following constraints:

N and R cannot both close.
If N stays open, then L must also stay open.
If R stays open, then M must also stay open.
L and R cannot both stay open.

12. Which one of the following could be a complete and accurate list of the stations that stay open?

(A)   L, M
(B)   P, R
(C)   M, N, Q
(D)   M, Q, R
(E)   L, M, P, R

GO ON TO THE NEXT PAGE.

13. If exactly five of the stations stay open, which one of the following must close?

  (A)   L
  (B)   M
  (C)   N
  (D)   P
  (E)   R

14. The stations that close could include both

  (A)   L and M
  (B)   L and R
  (C)   M and N
  (D)   M and R
  (E)   N and R

15. If L stays open, then any of the following could be true EXCEPT:

  (A)   M closes.
  (B)   N closes.
  (C)   M stays open.
  (D)   P stays open.
  (E)   Q stays open.

16. If exactly two of the stations stay open, which one of the following must close?

  (A)   L
  (B)   M
  (C)   N
  (D)   Q
  (E)   R

17. Which one of the following, if substituted for the constraint that if R stays open, then M must also stay open, would have the same effect in determining which stations close and which stay open?

  (A)   If L closes, then M must stay open.
  (B)   If L closes, then R must stay open.
  (C)   If R closes, then L must stay open.
  (D)   If L stays open, then M must close.
  (E)   If M stays open, then N must close.

GO ON TO THE NEXT PAGE.

Questions 18–23

An environmental consultant will examine the air quality on eight floors of an office tower, the first floor to the eighth floor. Each floor will be examined on one of four consecutive days—Wednesday, Thursday, Friday, and Saturday—with exactly two floors being examined on each day. The following conditions apply:

On any given day, the two floors examined must be separated by at least one other floor.

The second floor must be examined on an earlier day than the eighth floor.

The third floor must be examined on an earlier day than the seventh floor.

The seventh floor must be examined on an earlier day than the fifth floor.

The fourth floor must be examined on either Thursday or Friday.

18. Which one of the following assignments of floors to the first two days could be part of an acceptable schedule for all four days?

(A) Wednesday: first floor, third floor
Thursday: sixth floor, eighth floor

(B) Wednesday: first floor, sixth floor
Thursday: second floor, third floor

(C) Wednesday: second floor, fourth floor
Thursday: third floor, eighth floor

(D) Wednesday: second floor, sixth floor
Thursday: fourth floor, eighth floor

(E) Wednesday: third floor, sixth floor
Thursday: second floor, seventh floor

GO ON TO THE NEXT PAGE.

19. If the third floor is examined on Thursday, which one of the following could be true?

   (A)   The first floor is examined on Saturday.
   (B)   The second floor is examined on Friday.
   (C)   The sixth floor is examined on Thursday.
   (D)   The seventh floor is examined on Thursday.
   (E)   The eighth floor is examined on Friday.

20. Any of the following could be true EXCEPT:

   (A)   The first floor is examined on Friday.
   (B)   The third floor is examined on Thursday.
   (C)   The fifth floor is examined on Thursday.
   (D)   The sixth floor is examined on Saturday.
   (E)   The eighth floor is examined on Friday.

21. The schedule for the air-quality examination is fully determined if which one of the following is true?

   (A)   The second floor is examined on Friday.
   (B)   The third floor is examined on Thursday.
   (C)   The fifth floor is examined on Friday.
   (D)   The sixth floor is examined on Thursday.
   (E)   The eighth floor is examined on Thursday.

22. If the fifth floor is examined on Friday, which one of the following must be true?

   (A)   The first floor is examined on Wednesday.
   (B)   The first floor is examined on Saturday.
   (C)   The second floor is examined on Thursday.
   (D)   The second floor is examined on Friday.
   (E)   The eighth floor is examined on Friday.

23. Which one of the following, if substituted for the condition that the fourth floor must be examined on either Thursday or Friday, would have the same effect in determining the schedule for the air-quality examination?

   (A)   The fourth floor and the seventh floor must be examined either on the same day as each other or on consecutive days.
   (B)   The fourth floor cannot be examined on an earlier day than the second floor or on a later day than the eighth floor.
   (C)   The fourth floor must be examined on an earlier day than the fifth floor.
   (D)   If the fourth floor is not examined on Thursday, the seventh floor must be examined on Thursday.
   (E)   If the third floor is examined on Thursday, the fourth floor must be examined on Friday.

S T O P

IF YOU FINISH BEFORE TIME IS CALLED, YOU MAY CHECK YOUR WORK ON THIS SECTION ONLY.
DO NOT WORK ON ANY OTHER SECTION IN THE TEST.

Acknowledgment is made to the following sources from which material has been adapted for use in this test booklet:

Marjorie K. M. Chan and Douglas W. Lee, "Chinatown Chinese: A Linguistic and Historical Re-evaluation" in *Amerasia Journal*. ©1981 by Marjorie K. M. Chan and Douglas W. Lee.

Emmanuelle Fauchart and Eric von Hippel, "Norms-Based Intellectual Property Systems: The Case of French Chefs" in *Organization Science*. ©2008 by INFORMS.

Alejandro Jenkins and Gilad Perez, "Looking for Life in the Multiverse: Universes with Different Physical Laws Might Still Be Habitable" in *Scientific American*. ©2010 by *Scientific American*, a division of Nature American, Inc.

Ann J. Lane, Introduction to *Herland*. ©1979 by Ann J. Lane.

Dotan Oliar and Christopher Jon Sprigman, "There's No Free Laugh (Anymore): The Emergence of Intellectual Property Norms and the Transformation of Stand-Up Comedy" in *Virginia Law Review*. ©2008 by Virginia Law Review.

Wait for the supervisor's instructions before you open the page to the topic.
Please print and sign your name and write the date in the designated spaces below.
Time: 35 Minutes

General Directions

ou will have 35 minutes in which to plan and write an essay on the topic inside. Read the topic and the accompanying directions carefully. ou will probably find it best to spend a few minutes considering the topic and organizing your thoughts before you begin writing. In your essay, e sure to develop your ideas fully, leaving time, if possible, to review what you have written. **Do not write on a topic other than the one** ecified. **Writing on a topic of your own choice is not acceptable.**

special knowledge is required or expected for this writing exercise. Law schools are interested in the reasoning, clarity, organization, nguage usage, and writing mechanics displayed in your essay. How well you write is more important than how much you write.

nfine your essay to the blocked, lined area on the front and back of the separate Writing Sample Response Sheet. Only that area will be produced for law schools. Be sure that your writing is legible.

Both this topic sheet and your response sheet must be turned in to the testing staff before you leave the room.

Topic Code	Print Your Full Name Here		
154380	Last	First	M.I.

Date	Sign Your Name Here
/ /	

Scratch Paper
Do not write your essay in this space.

LSAT® Writing Sample Topic

Directions: The scenario presented below describes two choices, either one of which can be supported on the basis of the information given. Your essay should consider both choices and argue for one over the other, based on the two specified criteria and the facts provided. There is no "right" or "wrong" choice: a reasonable argument can be made for either.

Kate Li is an independent journalist who publishes stories on a small, ad-supported Internet news website that she owns and manages. She has received an anonymous tip that a prominent political campaign has been covertly violating campaign finance laws. Li must decide whether to publish the story on her website or pass the tip on to a larger news organization. Using the facts below, write an essay in which you argue for one option over the other based on the following two criteria:

- Li wants to further her career as a journalist.
- Li wants to promote the business interests of her news website.

If Li publishes the story on her website she will receive sole journalistic credit for the story. Li lacks the resources to thoroughly vet the anonymous tip herself before publishing the story. An unvetted story must be acknowledged as unverified if it is published. Publishing unverified stories is considered unprofessional for journalists unless the public would otherwise fail to get valuable information. News stories about political corruption are widely shared on Internet sites and social media. Publishing stories that are widely shared greatly increases the number of people visiting a news website. Journalists with a reputation for publishing unverified stories receive significantly more anonymous tips than journalists who do not have such a reputation.

Political stories published by large news organizations achieve high visibility in a variety of media. These organizations occasionally share journalistic credit with independent journalists who pass along tips for stories. Stories about political corruption sometimes result in lawsuits against publications and journalists. Large news organizations retain legal staff to support their stories and sources. Many large news organizations maintain reciprocal relationships with smaller news outlets, trading smaller scale stories in exchange for tips on stories with a larger scope.

WPAB

Scratch Paper
Do not write your essay in this space.

LAST NAME (Print)

FIRST NAME (Print)

LAST 4 DIGITS OF SOCIAL SECURITY/SOCIAL INSURANCE NO.

L

LSAC ACCOUNT NO.

MI

TEST CENTER NO.

SIGNATURE

M M D D Y Y
TEST DATE

TOPIC CODE

Writing Sample Response Sheet

DO NOT WRITE IN THIS SPACE

**Begin your essay in the lined area below.
Continue on the back if you need more space.**

COMPUTING YOUR SCORE

Directions:

1. Use the Answer Key on the next page to check your answers.

2. Use the Scoring Worksheet below to compute your raw score.

3. Use the Score Conversion Chart to convert your raw score into the 120–180 scale.

Scoring Worksheet

1. Enter the number of questions you answered correctly in each section.

	Number Correct
SECTION I.................	_____
SECTION II...............	_____
SECTION III..............	_____
SECTION IV	_____

2. Enter the sum here: _____

This is your Raw Score.

Conversion Chart
For Converting Raw Score to the 120–180 LSAT Scaled Score
LSAT Form 7LSN126

Reported Score	Raw Score Lowest	Raw Score Highest
180	99	101
179	98	98
178	97	97
177	96	96
176	95	95
175	94	94
174	93	93
173	92	92
172	91	91
171	90	90
170	89	89
169	87	88
168	86	86
167	84	85
166	83	83
165	81	82
164	79	80
163	77	78
162	76	76
161	74	75
160	72	73
159	70	71
158	69	69
157	67	68
156	65	66
155	63	64
154	62	62
153	60	61
152	58	59
151	57	57
150	55	56
149	54	54
148	52	53
147	50	51
146	49	49
145	47	48
144	46	46
143	44	45
142	43	43
141	41	42
140	40	40
139	38	39
138	37	37
137	35	36
136	34	34
135	32	33
134	31	31
133	30	30
132	29	29
131	27	28
130	26	26
129	25	25
128	24	24
127	23	23
126	22	22
125	21	21
124	20	20
123	19	19
122	18	18
121	17	17
120	0	16

ANSWER KEY

SECTION I

1.	C	8.	E	15.	E	22.	A
2.	D	9.	A	16.	C	23.	C
3.	A	10.	C	17.	B	24.	B
4.	C	11.	A	18.	E	25.	C
5.	C	12.	A	19.	A		
6.	D	13.	C	20.	D		
7.	A	14.	B	21.	B		

SECTION II

1.	C	8.	D	15.	B	22.	E
2.	C	9.	D	16.	B	23.	A
3.	E	10.	C	17.	E	24.	D
4.	A	11.	C	18.	D	25.	B
5.	A	12.	B	19.	A	26.	B
6.	A	13.	E	20.	B	27.	A
7.	B	14.	C	21.	D		

SECTION III

1.	C	8.	D	15.	D	22.	B
2.	E	9.	C	16.	B	23.	C
3.	C	10.	E	17.	E	24.	C
4.	A	11.	D	18.	A	25.	A
5.	E	12.	D	19.	D	26.	D
6.	B	13.	E	20.	D		
7.	A	14.	C	21.	D		

SECTION IV

1.	D	8.	E	15.	B	22.	D
2.	C	9.	A	16.	D	23.	A
3.	B	10.	E	17.	A		
4.	B	11.	B	18.	E		
5.	C	12.	D	19.	A		
6.	D	13.	E	20.	C		
7.	B	14.	D	21.	E		

LSAT® PREP TOOLS

The Official LSAT SuperPrep II™

SuperPrep II contains everything you need to prepare for the LSAT—a guide to all three LSAT question types, three actual LSATs, explanations for all questions in the three practice tests, answer keys, writing samples, and score-conversion tables, plus invaluable test-taking instructions to help with pacing and timing. SuperPrep has long been our most comprehensive LSAT preparation book, and SuperPrep II is even better. The practice tests in SuperPrep II are PrepTest 62 (December 2010 LSAT), PrepTest 63 (June 2011 LSAT), and one test that has never before been disclosed.

With this book you can

- Practice on genuine LSAT questions
- Review explanations for right and wrong answers
- Target specific categories for intensive review
- Simulate actual LSAT conditions

LSAC sets the standard for LSAT prep—and SuperPrep II raises the bar!

Available at your favorite bookseller.

LSAC.org